FRENCH HEROINES

FRENCH HEROINES
1940-1945

Courage, Strength and Ingenuity

by
Monique Saigal

Printed in the USA, 2010.
Front Cover: Photo of **Rivka Leiba**

additional copies
jacabr@aol.com

Dedicated to my grandmother Rivka Leiba,
who died in Auschwitz in 1942,
and to my father, Aaron Ségal,
who died in the trenches in 1940.

To Steve and
Karen
This book honors
very courageous women
who took many ways
in order to fight against
the Nazi Occupant.
Best/
Troiene
Oct 4. 2012

"We have fought for our just cause; we will fight to the end. If we fall, it will be in combat, with dignity and pride, not out of cowardice or despair."

Marie-Jo Chombart de Lauwe

TABLE OF CONTENTS

Foreword	3
Introduction	7
A Courageous Leader	15
Interview with Maïti Girtanner (July 17, 2003)	15
The Jewish Resistance Fighters	29
Interview with Liliane Klein-Lieber (July 22, 2002)	29
Interview with Yvette Farnoux (June 12, 2003)	39
Interview with Huguette Prety (June 22, 2002)	45
Interview with Andrée Warlin (June 17, 2002)	49
Interview with Marthe Cohn (August 2, 2002)	57
The Resistance Fighters of "Défense de la France"	71
Interview with Hélène Viannay (July 3, 2003)	71
Interview with Jacqueline Pardon (July 3, 2002)	77
Interview with Jacqueline Marié Fleury (July 1, 2002)	85
The Resistance Fighters of London's BCRA	
(Bureau of Air Force Operations)	95
Interview with Brigitte Friang (July 22, 2001)	95
Interview with Jeanne Bohec (June 26, 2001)	103
The Communist Resistance Fighters	109
Interview with Raymonde Tillon (June 27, 2002)	109
Interview with Henriette Kermann.(June 13, 2002)	117
The "Alibi" Network	127
Interview with Claire Richet (June 27, 2003)	127
A Lifelong Commitment	133
Interview with Lucie Aubrac (July 5, 2001)	133
A Civic Duty	143
Interview with Noëlla Rouget (July 12, 2002)	143
Once a Fighter, Always a Fighter	153
Interview with Marie-Jo Chombart de Lauwe (July 8, 2002)	153
My Grandmother Rivka Leiba	165
Means of Survival	167
Acknowledgments	175
Bibliography	177

FRENCH HEROINES, 1940-1945

FOREWORD

History is a link between the living and the dead. Today, the horizon looms before us: soon, the witnesses will be gone. But up to the last day, we must keep alive the dialog about a past which haunts our present. Unfortunately, quite often, the judgments expressed in and by the public share two complementary features: ignorance of the facts and a tendency to generalize and simplify.

The Resistance was not built by men alone. Maurice Schumann, Radio London's voice for Free France, declared on the air in 1943 that, "for the first time in this war, women have given hundreds of millions of fighters"[1]

This book serves as a reminder of that fact; in addition, its various viewpoints provide us with a clearer picture of what the Resistance was: diverse, ever-evolving, thought-through and spontaneous, generous, terribly dangerous, agonizing...

It was built by humans and it was ever-mobile. This book also reminds us that the so-called "Resistance values"—sense of honor, altruism, giving of oneself and selflessness—were also shared by both genders, although society has not recognized that in its major portrayals. Thus, among the 1038 Companions of the Liberation, there are only 6 women.

What is a 20-year-old to do after this colossal military defeat of 1940, after the occupation and the establishment of the so-called Vichy regime?

Is silence an appropriate response?

Indeed, it can possibly—and fleetingly—be construed as a weapon of resistance and no submission. A considerable number

---

[1] He was aware, however, that throughout history, women have always held an active role in supporting resistance movements against occupying forces.

of people, for various reasons, persuaded themselves of its eloquence. It is an expression of dignity, perfectly described by Vercors in his book, *The Silence of the Sea,* written in 1941, clandestinely published and distributed in the free zone starting in 1942. Through the story of a young woman and her uncle who are forced to share their home with a French-speaking German officer, the narrative makes absolute muteness a weapon defending honor.

This line of conduct, however, is sorely tested by the violence of the real world. How can one resist, or rather, continue to fight? For, early on, that is how these young women formulate the question. As Lucie Aubrac, the first woman to sit on the Consultative Assembly of Algiers, put it, "The Germans who threatened women and asphyxiated children made this war women's business as well."

Their involvement, along with that of men, was unequivocally essential to the historiography of a France undergoing rebirth. In other words, a minority of French people made it appear as if the Resistance had been a countrywide collective undertaking. Reflection on guilt was replaced by mystical allegory. It was as if, wrote Paul Thibault in the magazine *Esprit,* the courage of a significant minority could be attributed to France.

Yet, paradoxically, France chronicled thousands of simple and selfless deeds, all of which are also true acts of resistance. For example, the chance meeting, on the Dax train station platform on August 24th, 1942, of Jacqueline de Saint-Quentin Baleste and a little girl with long blond hair wearing a red dress. The little girl was holding the hand of a slightly older boy because she needed someone to hang on to. She had arrived from Paris and it was six weeks after the Vél d'Hiv roundup. She was Jewish and her grandmother had wanted to keep her from being arrested. Jacqueline, sixty-five years later and now honored as a "Juste de France" (the honorary title of "Righteous" for having rescued Jews during the war), continues just as tenderly to hold the hand of Monique Saigal, the author of this book.

A book which raises two essential questions: Can certain kinds of suffering ever end? Forgiveness, "that sinister joke," as Vladimir Jankelevitch declared, "did it not die in the camps?"

It takes exceptional force of character to absolve one's executioner, even decades later, when he is on his deathbed, contrite and repentant. Yet, as Monique Saigal reveals, Maïti Girtanner overcame her suffering and found the courage to forgive the unforgivable. In the name of God, presented by Bossuet as "the only one worthy of avenging crimes…"

Henri Weill

FRENCH HEROINES, 1940-1945

INTRODUCTION

Women in the French Resistance: Here are the stories of eighteen women who are little known yet who stand out because of their extraordinary courage during the German occupation in World War II, when they risked their lives, engaging in clandestine activities to overcome the Nazis. Why eighteen? Because the number eighteen ("chai" in Hebrew) stands for life, which they gave back to persecuted innocents. These women are the splendid embodiment of the spiritual meaning of that number. Catholic, Jewish, and Protestant, they transcend religions in the name of a common ideal. As Mme Noëlla Rouget says, "There is no race but the human race."

A "hidden child" of the Holocaust taken in by a Catholic family in 1942, I wrote this book to honor these courageous, ingenious women, as well as my grandmother, who perished at Auschwitz. Eager to discover the secrets of the women in the Resistance, such as Lucie Aubrac, I crisscrossed France, Switzerland, and California to hear them tell their own stories. My goal in this book is to make these women and their courageous deeds known to the English-speaking audience. Reading these texts takes us back to a time of terror when women fought back with every ounce of strength and wit at their disposal. What a splendid example they provide for today's youth who are searching for meaning in their lives!

Ordinary individuals before World War II, the war was a catalyst that accelerated and revealed in these women a strength of character, courage, and extraordinary inventiveness determined to overcome the Nazi enemy. The women of the French Resistance featured in this book hid people pursued by the

7

Gestapo, worked as spies, taught young French soldiers how to make explosives, coded and decoded messages, prayed, and served as nurses and social workers, in addition to performing the "feminine work" (chores) expected of women. At Ravensbruck, the concentration camp where many of them were sent to do hard work for Germany with hardly anything to eat or drink, they continued to resist the Nazi enemy by engaging in clandestine and dangerous activities, such as mixing bad and small parts, breaking the machinery, or slowing down production. Some did not hesitate to use insolence and shrewdness, lies and even theft, as well as feminine seduction, to get their way. Solidarity of purpose was a means of survival. All of the women viewed their actions as normal and natural in extraordinary, hellish times.

On July 16 and 17, 1942, the dates of the Vel'd'Hiv in Paris, the Germans rounded up more than 13,000 Jews, both adults and children, to be sent to Auschwitz. One month later, on August 24, 1942, when I was 3 years old, my grandmother, fearing for my life, threw me in a train carrying young children whose fathers, like mine, had died in the war. The children were to spend a one-month vacation with host families in Southwest France. The convoy was organized by a state organization, "the House of the Prisoner," to help war widows. When I arrived at my destination, no one was there to greet me since I was not registered. However, a young 20 year-old woman named Jacqueline Baleste, who had come with her father, an injured veteran of World War I, to pick up a 4 year-old boy, saw me in tears. She came near me, took me in her arms, and asked the Mayor of Dax in charge of the convoy if she could take me, since the little boy did not show up. He accepted. She later told me, "I immediately became attracted to you; you were so cute."

When we came to the car, I said, "We must wait for daddy." I did not understand my father was deceased, a casualty of the war. These were my last words before a long period during which I remained silent. Soon, I met the whole Baleste family in the small village of Luë. They welcomed me with joy. The house had a garden full of flowers and a farmyard with chickens and rabbits with whom I liked to have imaginary conversations.

I was scheduled to go back to Paris on September 26 to the great despair of the Baleste family who had become attached to me. However, a catastrophe involving my grandmother spared my life. One day prior, on September 25, 1942, the day of the raid of Romanian Jews in France, two French police knocked at the door of our apartment in the Jewish XXth district of Paris. They were coming to get my grandmother, Rivka Leiba, betrayed by her concierge, to take her to the Drancy internment camp. When she heard the ferocious pounding on the door, she asked her 19 year-old son, my Uncle Daniel, my mother's younger brother, who was in the apartment, to go hide in the back bedroom. My little 2 year -old sister was eating in the kitchen. My grandmother hurried out as quickly as possible, refusing to take anything with her so the police would not discover my uncle.

On September 30, 1942, my grandmother was gassed at Auschwitz.

While this tragedy was unfolding, Daniel contacted my mother who was working and told her the news about the raid. She immediately sent a telegram to the Baleste family, asking them if they could keep me a while longer and find a family for my sister. They did.

Since two German officers were living at the Baleste residence—inhabitants of the village had to give room and board to German soldiers—the Balestes asked my mother for permission to baptize me for more security. She accepted and I was raised Catholic. I went to Mass every Sunday. Once, during the war my mother came to visit me but was denounced as a Jew and fled rapidly on a bike.

I wanted so much for my mother to be the first Resistance Fighter I would write about in this book but, as an adult, when I asked her to talk to me about my father and my grandmother, she couldn't. She claimed that she had made great efforts to forget this painful period of her life, that she did not remember anything. I did manage to find out that she herself was hidden in Southern France for six months during the German occupation, that she used to transport weapons hidden in a baby carriage, and distributed them to the men and women of the French Resistance Movement.

It was not until 1950, five years after the war ended, that my mother came to pick me up, as well as my sister, who had been living with a widow in another village. My mother had remarried an American, and on the day of my departure from the Baleste family, I had the mumps, which I consider a metaphor of my refusal to hear and accept the authority of my new Jewish parents.

Back in Paris with my mother, it was difficult for me to adapt to my new family. Raised Catholic for more than eight years by the Balestes, now, at age 12, I could no longer go to Mass on Sundays but was expected to live the life of a Jew. Since I had not received a Jewish religious education, I felt frustrated, torn, and pulled in two directions. Since my stepfather's parents lived in the

United States, I immigrated there and later studied at the University of California, Los Angeles (UCLA) where I received my B.A., M.A., and Ph.D. in French Literature. For more than 45 years, I have been a Professor of French in the Department of Romance Languages at Pomona College in Claremont, California. I have offered courses in literary analysis (prose, poetry, and theater), the modern French novel, French films, and a multimedia class entitled "Paris: Myth or Reality." It has been a rewarding career mentoring some of the best undergraduate students in the United States.

Not until the early 1990s, on a beautiful summer evening in Paris after having completed some scholarly research at the National Library, I visited my Uncle Daniel and suddenly had a personal revelation. I asked Daniel about the Jewish raids and the day the French police came to our apartment to capture my grandmother in 1942. I then realized for the first time that I had been a "hidden" child during the war and that the Baleste family could have been arrested and killed for protecting a little Jewish girl. I had always thought that I had been sent to the countryside because my mother worked and could not take care of me. In a way, this visit at my uncle's was a real turning point in my personal life and in the discovery of my origins. For years, I had never spoken about my childhood, nor of my Jewish origin. I had pursued my professional career as a Professor of French at Pomona College, married, and reared two daughters of my own, but these painful memories related to World War II in France had been repressed.

I decided to contact a university professor in California, who specializes in working with hidden children of the Holocaust. The first time she met me, she said, "You still live a hidden life." That

11

sentence opened my eyes and began the process of freeing me from a heavy inner burden. In 1995, I had the opportunity and the privilege to honor the Baleste family at the Yad Vashem Memorial in Jerusalem. In 2007, my godmother, Jacqueline Baleste, the only survivor by then, received the Legion of Honor in France for her deeds of righteousness during World War II.

In 1999, I decided to tell my story, kept secret for years, to my French students enrolled in my "Paris: Myth or Reality" course. Two years later, I spent the summer of 2001 visiting several former internment camps in France, such as Drancy, Pithiviers, Beaune la Rolande, as well as Izieu, a town near Lyon where Jewish children had been placed for their safety, I walked through the streets of Oradour-sur-Glane, a village completely decimated by the Nazis. I filmed the former concentration camp of the Struthof in Alsace and spoke to people in the Protestant enclave of Chambon sur Lignon where inhabitants saved 5000 Jews.

I then wondered what I could do with all of this information. Moved and saddened by what I had seen and heard, I decided to concentrate on the activities of women in the French Resistance. I was going to interview women, instead of men, because they are usually less well-known and their clandestine methods of intrigue differ from those of men. Moreover, I wanted to honor my grandmother, my father, and my "Righteous ones", the Baleste family. Therefore, I did research in the National Library in Paris; I looked for names in the de Gaulle Foundation, as well as that of the Resistance; I consulted a rabbi; and I went to a publishing house that sells works by and on World War II Resistance Fighters.

I spent several summers interviewing and filming women who had fought against the enemy and whom I call "heroines" because of their courage, ingenuity, bold character, and noteworthy accomplishments. Presented in this volume are their stories of "l'histoire vivante" (living, vibrant history), including oral testimony in their own words. The deeds of these18 war heroes need to be shared so that they can be known and celebrated by the English-speaking public, as well as their native countrymen in France. One of my former Pomona College students, who lives with her family in Paris now, worked diligently on the English translation of this book, which was published first in French in 2008 by Editions du Rocher, entitled "Heroines francaises, 1940-1945: Courage, force et ingeniosite."

Monique Saigal
Claremont, California
November 2010

FRENCH HEROINES, 1940-1945

A COURAGEOUS LEADER
Interview with Maïti Girtanner (July 17, 2003)

On July 17th, I was in Bonnes, a small village near Poitiers. Here, Maïti Girtanner spends her summers in the "Vieux Logis", the Louis XIV-era home on the banks of the river Vienne that has belonged to her family for generations.

I had read her published story.[2]   She spent several months hidden away with seventeen other Resistance fighters, all of whom were tortured. She is the only survivor, but since 1944 she has endured irreversible physical damage from this atrociously traumatic experience. Her nervous system has been seriously affected, resulting in several prolonged hospital stays. To her utmost distress, this once highly gifted pianist can no longer play the piano. During our two-hour interview, she had to get up twice to take medication.

On August 25th, 1940, the Germans invaded the village in which her parents had settled after the exodus. They entered her family's garden. A "biblical" wrath overtook eighteen-year-old Maïti, and at that moment, she decided to join the Resistance. "Right away, I thought, 'something has to be done.' Luckily, I had my bicycle, which made it easy for me to get around. I knew German, so I could speak with the occupying soldiers, and my piano-playing enchanted them greatly. Some students and I immediately formed a Resistance group."

---

[2] *Résistance et Pardon*, published by *Vie Chrétienne* in 2003, was based on the transcript of a film with the same title which producer Michel Farin dedicated to Girtanner's story. It was broadcast in two parts by the television channel France 2, as part of the program "Le Jour du Seigneur" ("Day of the Lord").

Maïti created an escape channel to help people flee from the German Gestapo to England or North Africa. A river flowed at the foot of the "Vieux Logis," demarcating occupied France from Free France. Maïti's friends knew that she lived on the border of the two zones and asked her for help. Escapees from German camps arrived in Paris. She rented an apartment for them. "They needed to take a train from Paris to Châtellerault, where friends lent me a horse-drawn carriage which they left at the train station. I rode the 20 kilometers (12.5 miles) with the runaways and brought them home with me. I hid them in the service area of the property until nightfall, when they could enter the free zone." There was permanent danger in Bonnes, since two German officers occupied the room overlooking the river and continually roamed around the house.

Maïti had a boat, which she brought to a bend in the river, out of the Germans' sight. "I would take the person I wanted to save and have him lie down at the bottom of the boat, covered with a cloth. I rowed to where the river turned, and beyond the bend, the Germans could no longer see me. When I had groups, we walked through the fields to the bend, and we swam across. After 5 kilometers (3 miles), we were in the free zone and they were safe."

A pass was mandatory to be able to travel by boat. Maïti went to Bonnes to see the Captain, who sent her to his superior officer. "No way," said the Major, "Go see the Colonel." She biked the 20 kilometers (12.5 miles) to the Prefecture of Poitiers. She opened the door of the large sitting room without knocking, shocking the Colonel. In her most elegant German, Maïti explained her request. "I am Swiss; I live in the village of Bonnes. I am studying for my exams—which was not true—and my teachers are in Chauvigny, in the free zone. I have come to ask your permission to cross the line of demarcation frequently to be able to speak with my teachers as well as simply to cross the river to the German side. There are eighteen of us living in my house, and I never have a moment of peace."

The Colonel refused. Maïti insisted, using another ploy. "I came to see you because I trust you and I think that you will understand my situation. I absolutely must pursue my career; I am a pianist." Won over, the Colonel gave her a one-month pass, which was not enough. Maïti asked again. In the end, the Colonel exclaimed, "You are quite bothersome! For the pleasure of never seeing you in my office again, I will give you an unlimited pass."

At 18, but appearing 15, with a black velvet bow in her blond curls, she seemed very innocent. Maïti proceeded not only to escort hundreds of people into the free zone, but also to transfer mail and money to sustain the Resistance network. The money was brought to a family in Chauvigny. "I became known to the large networks with high visibility in the free zone, where they had headquarters. They were only too happy to have someone willing to risk her life to help them. I would spend four days in Paris and then Friday, Saturday and Sunday in Bonnes. I would take the train and each time I would come back with one or two people who wanted to reach the free zone."

Since the escaped prisoners had neither ID cards nor food ration cards, Maïti began to make false ones. "I have an innate gift for copying and in Paris, through some connections, I met a printer who agreed to print fake cards." The Occupation was spreading its tentacles. At the beginning, 400 Germans occupied the village; that figure soon reached 800. Almost no one could be trusted. One day, an officer who liked Maïti and had an inkling of what she was doing, advised her to leave. She understood and did so. Another time, a pastor gave her the same advice, and she traveled further once again.

Maïti was sometimes in contact with General de Gaulle, who sent her orders through Geoffroy de Courcel. De Gaulle informed Maïti that some submarines were being repaired near Nantes, without any further explanation. "So I went to Nantes with a group of ten people to see them. Indeed, damaged submarines would arrive there for repairs and leave on a certain day. Three days before their departure—this was standard procedure—the officers came to bring their laundry and their uniforms to be cleaned in the city, 3 kilometers (1.9 miles) away. This gave me the idea of renting a van, which I called "Teinturerie Mésange" (Little Bird Cleaners), which we set up in their path. As I was the only one who spoke German, I stopped the first aide-de-camp I saw and said to him, 'To get to the dry cleaner's in the city, you must walk 3 kilometers, whereas we are trained professionals. We are cheaper, and we work fast and very well.'"

The Germans gave their clothes to Maïti's group to launder without removing their unit number or submarine name from their uniforms. Each time, they came from a different ship that would leave three days later. "I had a connection with a very large network that had the use of a radio and they warned the British that in three days, such-and-such submarine was leaving for Pas-de-Calais in the north. They were then sunk or damaged." She did this for several months, then she left. Another group took over for three years. Later, when she was arrested, she learned that the Germans had discovered the roots of the network and knew that she had initiated this activity.

Since she spoke English well, she was often asked to hide British fighters who had accidentally landed in the occupied zone. At the beginning, she hid them in the wine cellar of the house, among the straw bales. After a while, the German officers began to search the service area so she had to hide the British fighters in the adjoining woods.

In Paris, she heard about a wounded Englishman who wanted to reach England via the French free zone. She hid him in her rented apartment, where a friend of hers tended to his wounds. Once he felt better, she decided to take him on the train. "When I saw my Englishman, who was 300% English, standing out like a sore thumb with his red hair and freckles—so typically British, and wounded to boot—I panicked." She decided to pretend he was sick, since the Germans were so scared of germs. She wrapped his nose and mouth in a bright red muffler, so that only his eyes were visible. She warned him, "As soon as a German comes near you, start coughing, hacking and blowing your nose." When the Germans arrived in their compartment, she greeted them in German, showed them her papers and said, "Your job is really a thankless one; you must be tired of it." Meanwhile, the Englishman played the sick man. The inspectors whispered to Maïti, "Who is that guy?" She answered, "That gentleman got on when I did. I exchanged a few words with him and he told me he had tuberculosis." The inspectors rushed off without verifying his documents. Upon their arrival in Bonnes, the German soldiers at the train station checkpoint asked the Englishman for his papers. She explained that he was her cousin, adding, "He is ill; we fear it may be tuberculosis. He came here for the healing country air." The Germans shooed them away, "Go on, Miss Maïti, go on!"

Another time, she hid an Englishman on a path that was

patrolled constantly by the Germans. She forbade him to smoke, for "cigarettes smell!" But his nervousness made it impossible to resist a cigarette, and while Maïti was preparing the boat for him, she was approached by a German officer. He had caught the scent of cigarette smoke. "Miss Maïti, we are going on a man hunt. It'll be very exciting. Get on your bicycle and come with us," he invited her. What could she do? She knew that it always took them 45 minutes to get started. She ran as fast as she could towards the Englishman. "You are risking your life, but also mine and that of my family!" She told him to race down the hill so she could put him on her boat. But when she arrived at the river bend, he was nowhere in sight. After a search, she finally found him cowering on the ground in the field, crying, "I can't go on; I'll just face the firing squad." She exclaimed, "They'll shoot you, all right, and me and my whole household along with you!" She managed to lift him up and haul him onto the boat, covering him with the cloth. When they arrived in the middle of the river, the Germans shouted, "Have you seen any men hidden over there?" She said no, and suggested they take another path because "the river is too dangerous." She reached the French side and asked that someone come pick up her passenger, barely making it before the Germans came back. That was a frighteningly close call!

This Englishman and his wife came back to see Maïti several years after the war. He told her "it had made him sick to think that a nineteen-year-old girl had risked so much to save his life and deceive the enemy."

One day, a German officer asked her if she would play at a musical evening. She hesitated, but felt protected by her Swiss citizenship. "I also wanted to make a good impression. If I had refused, I risked getting into big trouble." She accepted and they were delighted.

FRENCH HEROINES, 1940-1945
Interview with Maïti Girtanner (July 17, 2003)

Some time later, the Germans were organizing a musical birthday party for the head of the Gestapo in Paris, Oberg, who was living in Paris at the Hotel Majestic. The conservatory recommended Maïti, "less for my talent than for my citizenship, which protected me," she told me modestly. "They did not want to endanger their French students." An officer announced to Maïti that he would come to pick her up the next day at 8 o'clock. "You will play for General Oberg." She immediately refused. "I am eighteen and a half; girls my age do not go out at night." But there was no way out; it was an order.

The piano before her was exquisite. "I was truly happy to be playing an instrument of such magnificence, and then I came to my senses." She looked at the general with a slightly cocky air and asked if he had enjoyed the recital. He had. Maïti then added, "Would you please give me my reward?" Oberg exclaimed with surprise, "Give you a reward?! When you have the honor of playing before the crème de la crème of German officers?" Maïti interrupted, "General, it is not money I am asking for. You spend your time arresting young so-called Resistance fighters who have never done anything wrong. They are studying for their exams, either at the conservatory or at the university. They are not even thinking about you. You arrest them and they can no longer study. All I am asking is that you release three or four of them, and that's it." Maïti had prepared the names. The day before, the general had arrested four major Resistance fighters. The next day, Maïti's companions were freed. Over the course of three and a half years, she played for the Germans five or six times, each time making the same request. She thus obtained the release of several Resistance fighters.

Nevertheless, the fatal day came. Maïti was arrested in Paris, "completely by accident." She had been staying in a small cabin in the corner of her friends' garden. "There were nineteen Resistance fighters hidden in the villa." One evening, she came home on her bicycle. The Germans were in front of the gate, arresting everyone who was going in. Maïti was taken to the Gestapo counter-intelligence headquarters on avenue Foch, where she was first interrogated. She had been locked up for ten days when General Oberg came and recognized her. "That's our little Swiss friend. Release her immediately!" The Captain enumerated the list of Maïti's activities: Amiens, Nantes, money transfers, messages, escaped prisoners, Englishmen saved, boats sunk. The general exploded, "'She's a terrorist! Bring her to me now!' He was blood-red with wrath! He began to scream preposterous things. 'It's shameful, criminal! You deserve to die, but I am sentencing you to a punishment—which, as you know, is torture.' My fate was sealed. The next day, I was taken away in a car with darkened windows to a vast estate that had been transformed into a retaliation camp. The Germans were using it to break German soldiers who refused to obey. It was very isolated. People heard screams from time to time. They grabbed me and threw me into a basement with seventeen other people, men and women."

Five German doctors lived in the camp. Their mission was to punish those who resisted. One of the doctors kept them inside, against the door. Since he never stepped away from Maïti, she tried to establish "a sort of equal footing." She asked him his name and age. His name was Leo and he was 26 years old. She asked how he had come to take on this role of doctor-torturer. He had been chosen at a young age by Hitler to study advanced neurosurgery. "His chest swelled with pride; he was very proud.

Inflicting suffering was revenge for the evil that the 'Resistant terrorists' were bringing upon the great Germany. They had to be punished, and, above all, eliminated."

Maïti and her companions were in Leo's hands. She was the youngest. They lay prostrate against the wall in a cement basement, with only one thin article of clothing on their backs. Sometimes they received food and water, and other times they did not. The Germans took them away, one after the other, to get information out of them and to cause them the greatest possible pain. They destroyed "I don't know what," she, said, "so that human beings ended up dying of suffering; their hearts gave out." They beat her with iron bars and wooden clubs.

Maïti quickly noticed that her companions were showing worrisome signs. So she pronounced a phrase that she still remembers to this day and that had nothing to do with their sinister circumstances. She said, "I like hound hunting." She had followed hunting parties in her childhood. Her companions then started to talk about what they liked, building up a sort of fraternity. "A bond was created between us." When one of them came back in a pitiful state, the others comforted him or her.

Maïti's second intervention was spiritual, because, one by one, they were dying. She spoke again: "I do not need to know if you have a religion or not. I am a practicing Catholic, and I pray every day. I think that now is the time for us to pray to God to help us die well, since it seems that we cannot escape death." She set aside fifteen minutes each day for prayer. Some people prayed with her; others did not, but towards the end, all of the survivors united in prayer. It was a strong source of sustenance.

Maïti had long conversations with the torturer, Leo. She told him repeatedly, "What you are doing is horrendous!" He replied that the treatment inflicted upon them would serve as an example and dissuade terrorists. Maïti explained to him what the Resistance stood for. She told him that the occupants had misconstrued it, and that what they were doing was perverse. Those who resisted were giving their lives to free their country, while the Germans were doing it to conquer. According to Maïti, this German had to admit that the French were doing the right thing.

Maïti believes that if she had had two more months, she would have succeeded in winning him over. "I had tried to tell him to run away, to hide, to go back to Germany because what he was doing was criminal." She felt that she had succeeded in unsettling him, even though he continued to torture them.

When she saw him after the war, he said to her, "How was it possible that at such a young age your words were so powerful, so true and relevant to your situation?"

At the beginning of the Resistance, Maïti had told her older brother and the Swiss minister in Paris that she would send word every Wednesday. If they did not hear from her, that meant she had been caught. They sent French teams to look for her, but Maïti was nowhere to be found. In February 1944, the Swiss minister, a childhood friend of her father, gathered a group of friends. They figured out that the Resistance fighters who had been interrogated at the Gestapo headquarters on avenue Foch had not been sent to Germany, but had either been shot or disappeared. They searched in northern, eastern and western France, and then moved gradually south. The search went on for two months. They decided to speak to the bakers who distributed bread to various locations. One day, having heard some noise in a villa, they spoke to the local baker. "Yes, I deliver mainly to the villas and to a very large castle four kilometers (2.5 miles) from here, where I bring a lot of bread. Each time I deliver the ten kilos of bread, I hear screams. There must be dreadful things going on there." One evening, a member of the Swiss group courageously snuck into the castle's park. He looked into the basement windows. One of them seemed to be lit. He came back during the day, and saw two faces, one of which was possibly Maïti's. "Then they did all they could to tell the French Resistance. They created a large action group and invaded the property. Leo was finishing me off at that moment. There were two other prisoners in the basement, doctors who later committed suicide. The Swiss saved us. I had almost lost consciousness." Of the five German doctor-torturers, three were arrested and two escaped into the countryside, including Leo, who then went back to Germany.

Maïti, very near death and with shattered bones, received medical treatment in Switzerland and was then hospitalized in France. "If you put all the hospital stays back to back—they were not all consecutive—they add up to eight years, including three consecutive years." Since she was strong, with a healthy constitution, she did her best to overcome the injuries. One of her first thoughts was to "do an inventory not of what I had lost, but of what still remained of my mental capacity." Her career as a pianist was over. She no longer had the necessary strength. She wanted to become a teacher, so she took all the exams in a wheelchair. Then she taught philosophy and theology courses. She wanted to help young people "stand up straight in their boots with a truly positive attitude." She could not teach in a lycée because any commute was physically impossible. So she went to see an inspector in Versailles and explained her case to him. He was astonished by her self-assurance, and authorized her to teach philosophy from home. At the beginning, he checked on her students every three months, but after the second year, she never saw him again. Her students passed the baccalauréat exam as independent candidates, and out of all the students she taught since 1950, only four failed the exam.

And then, one evening in 1984, out of the blue, the telephone rang. She answered and immediately recognized Leo's voice. He was in Paris, he was terminally ill, and he wanted to see her. He had little time left to live and he feared death. "In the basement, I often heard you speak to your fellow prisoners about death. You spoke of it so well. I sought you out because of that." What should she do? Should she see him? Everything inside her screamed, "No!" but "I heard myself say, 'Come tomorrow at 3 o'clock.'"

The next day, Leo and his wife came to see Maïti, who was lying down and could not get up. He did not dare approach her. She offered him a seat. "He sat down and lowered his head." She spoke to him, "Leo, you told me on the phone yesterday that you feared death. What is death for you?" Her former torturer replied, "Death, to me, is, for example, entering a garage that is closed off with an iron curtain and I am alone in there. There is only a little hole through which I see the world living, parents happily watching their children laugh and play; and I am locked in. I can no longer communicate in any way with them, for the rest of eternity." Maïti asked him if he believed in God. He admitted that he was Catholic, but having been raised in the Hitlerjugend (Hitler Youth), he had lost his faith. Hitler had become his god. Maïti explained to him that for her, "'God is everything. He is the one I came from and the one I am going towards, and you almost sent me to him. As you can see, I am lying down, thanks to you.' I did not want him to think that I was just going to pat him on the back, but on the other hand, I was very hospitable." For her, Life continues after death. "When the time comes to go to the other side, the road, instead of closing, broadens and we fall at the feet of God, who is all love, all mercy, and all forgiveness. And since the beginning of my life, I have been moving forward each day, a little bit closer to Him. I believe in Him. I know that He loves me."

Leo, the former SS, and Maïti, the former Resistance Fighter, talked about Jesus Christ. She told him how she had devoted her time to teaching young people, helping them get through life by giving them a solid education, from a practical and spiritual standpoint. Leo looked at her in despair "But, after everything I have done, how can you expect me to reach God?" She responded, "There is crime, but there is also an antidote to crime. To counter evil, there is good. He murmured, 'What, oh what is it?' and I replied, 'Love.' If you oppose it to all crimes, you will be saved.'" This man had grown very rich, was now a distinguished doctor, the mayor of his city, loved by all. "I told him, 'you have three months left to live, so live by love alone. Give as much love as you can to all those around you. Love is what helps us die and what helps us enter into the period of life where all will be nothing but love and forgiveness.'" At the word "forgiveness," Leo reacted. "Can you forgive?" Maïti stretched her hand towards him. "I put my hand on his hand. I squeezed it hard and said, 'Leo, I forgive you. I have forgiven you.' His face brightened as if lit up by the sun. I think I even saw a tear." Maïti confessed, "I spent my whole life trying to forgive you, you and the other doctors. I think I have done it."

She assured him that he was going to meet God, who would cleanse him of his crimes. Leo stood up. "He bent low to say goodbye to me and when he came up to me, since I was lying down, I held out my arms to him, took his head between my hands and kissed him on the forehead. He said 'Forgive me' in German and quickly left with his wife."

Two and a half months later, Leo was on his deathbed. His wife asked him if he wanted to see a doctor or a priest. He just had time to say "Maïti," and he died.

Between his last meeting with Maïti and his death, he had come clean before God. He had gathered his family and friends and had revealed his role as a doctor-torturer during the war. "He gave himself over to love," concluded Maïti. He had even given away a part of his wealth to the poor, in compliance with the laws of Christian charity.

Maïti's valor reached the quintessence of courage, the courage to forgive the unforgivable. She was deeply moved when she told me, "That literally turned me inside out. It was very painful physically. But at the same time, I had a feeling of accomplishment, as if, up to that time, I had lived only to meet him, to be able to talk to him and to say 'I have forgiven you.'" [3]

---

[3] Then she was interviewed on Jean-Marie Cavada's television show. "He asked very few questions, but I talked a lot, for an hour and a half, just like I am talking to you now. I was very natural, and I was able to say everything I wanted to say about philosophy, spirituality and forgiveness."

JEWISH RESISTANCE FIGHTERS
Interview with Liliane Klein-Lieber (July 22, 2002)

Liliane Klein-Lieber was born in 1924 in Strasbourg to a family of liberal Jews who had lived in the Alsace region for several generations. At the age of seven, Liliane joined the Eclaireurs Israélites de France (EIF), the French Jewish Scout movement founded in 1923 by Robert Gamzon.

With the rise of Nazism, the nine-year-old girl subconsciously sensed danger. "I overheard my parents listening to the radio, which broadcast Hitler's diatribes and his hatred of Jews." During the same period, her parents were hiding Jewish friends on the run from Germany.

When war was declared on September 3rd, 1939, the population of Strasbourg and the entire bank of the Rhine was evacuated. The Lieber family found refuge in Vichy, a spa town with housing and schools. The Vichy synagogue became the gathering place for young Jews, who created a scout group that Liliane joined. She continued her studies at the Cusset secondary school a few kilometers away. "During the May 1940 exodus, all of the young people of Vichy, including myself, took in refugees from the north of France and Belgium, who were running from German troops. France was divided into two zones." The Vichy government immediately enforced the Statute on Jews passed on October 3rd, 1940[4], expelling all foreigners from Vichy and from the entire Allier department. It was a harsh winter. Along with her

---

[4] According to the first "Statute on Jews," they could no longer work in the civil service: the administration, legal system, police, armed forces, school system, press, radio, moviemaking, theater, etc. (with the exception of war veterans).

peers, Liliane knitted "gloves and socks for captured soldiers who were cold."

In December, Liliane's family was forced out of Vichy despite their French citizenship. They went to Grenoble, which had fallen under Italian control when the Germans invaded the southern zone. "At first, it was an advantage because the Italians did not apply the same anti-Semitic policies as the Germans did. But the respite only lasted until September 1943, when the Germans invaded the region."

In August 1942, Liliane had organized a camp in the Alps for Jewish girls from several cities in the south of France. Unfortunately, shortly after the camp session ended, on August 26th, there was a huge roundup and many of the Jewish children's parents were arrested. "Robert Gamzon then gathered the leaders of our movement, the EIF (Jewish Scouts), in Moissac. The Jewish Scouts had opened a home for Jewish children there to help their families and mainly to take them away from the capital, as the threat of bombs hung over Paris."

During this big meeting, the Jewish Scouts decided to set up an underground rescue network for children whose parents were in danger of arrest or had already been arrested. The network was divided into six regions for the southern zone, with Paris constituting the northern zone. Each region was headed by a regional leader and one or two assistants. "The girls held the role of 'social workers.' For security, the children we hid did not know our true identities, but only our scout symbols or code names. I was thus known as Luciole (Firefly)."

FRENCH HEROINES, 1940-1945
Interview with Liliane Klein-Lieber (July 22, 2002)

The scout network was under the auspices of the UGIF
(General Union of French Jews)[5] , in its sixth section of youth
movements, which is the reason it was nicknamed "The Sixth."
Its main charges were adolescents, as children under 13 were
taken under the wing of the Children's Aid Society *(Œuvre de
Secours aux Enfants)*. Liliane's activities were varied. "First and
foremost, we had to find hiding places for the young people that
were entrusted to us, as well as creating false identity cards." Due
to the abrupt separation from their families, these children often
suffered and felt abandoned. They did not realize that their
parents' sacrifice was made out of love. Moreover, it was difficult
for these children to accept their new identity and "to appear to
forget their Jewishness."

How were hiding places found? "By word of mouth, through
people we could trust completely. There were all types of
contacts who helped in placement: in various scout movements, in
convents for girls and on farms for boys. There were even some
in the youth movement *Compagnons de France*[6], created by the
Vichy regime. Some of the Compagnons' group leaders were in
the Resistance. We were also helped by police chiefs, city hall
employees and anyone else who was willing and able to assist us
in manufacturing or finding false identity papers and real stamps."
Through the benevolent complicity of the Congregation of *Notre
Dame de Sion* in Grenoble, they were able to place girls as hired
help in families, with room and board. These families risked as
much as the girls they took under their protection.

---

[5] The General Union of French Jews, created by the Vichy government under German
orders, in order to control all Jews, was divided into sections by profession.
[6] This movement, whose aim was to make French youth "tough and disciplined,"
organized various field work and farming camps.

FRENCH HEROINES, 1940-1945
Interview with Liliane Klein-Lieber (July 22, 2002)

Liliane was able to find a place for a young, very religious Austrian, Jean-Jacques Singer, with the *Compagnons de France* in Annecy. The EIF (French Jewish Scout Movement) had made false papers for him, making him Alsatian, "since his foreign accent put him in jeopardy." The young man was appointed as a pig herder in the farthest corner of a large farm, so that he would have as few contacts as possible with people so as not to blow his cover. "When I went to see him, he would say to me, 'See, Luciole, I can no longer wear my tefillin[7], and now I'm a pig herder!' Poor Jean-Jacques! He must have joined the F.F.I.[8] afterwards, since we never heard from him again."

The EIF did not always have the help of well-placed and understanding individuals to obtain false papers. Sometimes the Scouts had to "find a way to pilfer the necessary materials, honorably and virtuously, mind you!" Among them were some "genuine artists" who made stamps using erasers, pieces of linoleum and razor blades. "For the identity cards, all we had to do at the time was pay the fee, buy the form, fill it out with a pen, stamp it in the right place and affix a photo." When it came to filling in the birth place, the heroic counterfeiters chose cities that had been destroyed by bombs, so as to make verification impossible.

Liliane visited the young people she had placed as often as possible, in order to remind them that they had a friend who cared. Also, food and textile coupons had to be renewed every month.

---

[7] Tefillin, or phylacteries, are small leather cubes containing Bible verses on parchment, which Jews wear on their forehead and left arm during prayers.
[8] French Forces of the Interior.

Another female scout and friend put Liliane in contact with the director of the *Secours national*[9] in Grenoble, Mr. Dormoy. "Thanks to his humanitarian work, this very discreet man had access to large stores of useful materials, such as shoes, pants, jackets and boots, for the city's social service offices. I was able to use some of them for 'my kids.'"

Some of the young people were able to attend boarding schools along with everyone else. On weekends and during vacations, however, when their peers went home to their families, they ended up alone. During the winter vacation of 1943-44, Liliane took them on a trip to the mountains near Grenoble. "Those few days were marvelous: snow, skiing, sledding and singing around the fireplace. We even tried to provide meals as close as possible to their families' traditions. To this day, they talk and reminisce about that vacation, and so do I!"

Some young Jews were escorted to Switzerland, which was taking in those under 16. "We made some of them younger in their identity papers so that they would not be sent back and risk being caught by German border guards who were on duty day and night." To take the children across the border, they used trustworthy guides. "There were some big crooks, who took a lot of money and then allowed their victims to fall into the hands of the Germans."

A few friends attempted border crossings themselves. Some were successful; others were less fortunate. George Loinger, the current president and senior member of the *Anciens de la Résistance Juive* (Veterans of the Jewish Resistance), "guided

---

[9] A vast national charity founded during WWI and given renewed powers in 1940 to coordinate all charitable agencies for the war effort, as well as for propaganda purposes [Translator's note].

many children and adults across the border. Sometimes, he went all the way to Geneva, where he contacted Jewish Organizations that were represented there, such as the Children's Aid Society and the World Jewish Congress. He brought large sums of money back to France, which was extremely dangerous. The money had been collected from American Jews by JOINT, the American Jewish Joint Distribution Committee (JDC), and had been smuggled into Switzerland. It was used to fund Jewish networks and pay for room and board for children hidden by these organizations."

In Switzerland, the children stayed in refugee camps for several days. If they had any family left, they were reunited with family members. Otherwise, they were placed with volunteer foster families or in children's homes created especially for them by the Swiss Jewish community.

Although many hidden children, including the author of this book, were happy in their adoptive families, some were beaten or mistreated. "Jean-Pierre Guéno, Publishing Manager for RadioFrance, in his moving work about hidden children, *Paroles d'Etoiles*[10], wrote that while their parents wore their tattoos on their arms, the children wore theirs in their minds." Indeed, many of these children were traumatized for life.

Once, Liliane went to pick up two children whose parents were to be deported, at the Rivesaltes camp (near the city of Perpignan, in the eastern Pyrénées mountains). This enormous internment camp for foreigners, most of whom were Jews, had a sinister atmosphere which was amplified by the region's harsh climate: cold, wet winters and extremely hot summers.

---

[10] Jean-Pierre Guéno. *Paroles d'étoiles, Mémoire d'enfants cachés 1939-1945*, Paris, Flammarion, 2004.

Interview with Liliane Klein-Lieber (July 22, 2002)

"Thousands of people were crammed into unsanitary barracks, infested by disease-carrying lice and fleas. They slept on straw on the ground. Families were separated: women and children on one side and men on the other. Their idleness demoralized them and made the situation unbearable."

Social workers and teachers were authorized to work in this camp as volunteers. Liliane knew one of them: Andrée Salomon. "A wonderful woman, the head of this group of 'volunteer internees.'" These remarkable young women took care of the children and their mothers during their severe ordeal, whose outcome would be even more grim: a trip to Drancy followed by deportation.

On an October day in 1943, Liliane entered the camp, which smelled of death. "I had walked by dozens of barracks to find Andrée Salomon. She was waiting for me outside a hut that served as an office for the volunteers. She gave me a mission: I was to leave the camp with two boys, ages 7 and 12, and take them to Perpignan, and then to Moissac. Their parents were probably being deported as we spoke. I was able to take them out of the camp without a hitch." In Perpignan, Liliane and the two disoriented children stayed in a hotel room. "I paid for the room the evening we arrived, and it was a good thing, since the next morning the boys had wet their sheets and we had to run. Poor children! In the train, we tried to keep a low profile. 'My boys' heads were shaved because of the lice, and they did not speak or understand French. But we miraculously reached Moissac, where the boys were warmly welcomed."

Liliane kept in touch with some of the hidden children. "At the time, I called them 'my children' or 'my kids.' Over the years, they became like brothers and sisters to me; our age difference was insignificant. Some have even become friends with my own children, and that brings me joy." Most of them immigrated to the USA, to Canada or elsewhere. A few others found family members or friends of their parents. Many of these hidden children settled in Israel, having no more family ties in Europe or anywhere else in the world. "Their gratitude and loyalty are particularly touching," says Liliane of those with whom she has remained connected.

I asked Liliane to talk about the Righteous among the Nations. "There were many in all classes of society, in all religions[11]. They took enormous risks. Many of them did not want to be thanked, feeling they had simply done 'their duty.' Without the Righteous, nothing would have been possible. You know, France was not just a country of collaborators. It was a country of Resistance fighters. Without many French people, we would not have managed to hide Jews. France is the only country that was able to save three quarters of its Jewish population during the war. Entire villages, such as Chambon-sur-Lignon[12] in the Cévennes region, observed the law of silence. They saved up to 5,000 Jews, both children and adults, not counting the Resistance fighters."

Liliane adds: "In the 1960s, the State of Israel created a medal—the only one for civilians—paying tribute to all of the non-Jews who jeopardized their own lives to save at least one life during the war of 1939-1945. They are called the Righteous. On the medal, the following maxim from the Talmud is engraved: 'Whoever saves one life, saves the entire world."

---

[11] On this topic, see the book by Gay Block and Malka Drucker. *Rescuers: of Moral Courage in the Holocaust*. New York. London: Holmes & Meier Publishers, Inc. 1992.
[12] Pierre Sauvage, a filmmaker born in Chambon in 1943 paid tribute to the inhabitants of this village in his film, *Weapons of the Spirit* (1989).

FRENCH HEROINES, 1940-1945
Interview with Liliane Klein-Lieber (July 22, 2002)

Liliane, although often asked for her identity papers, was never arrested. It goes without saying that her gut often tightened with fear, as was the case for everyone at the time. The hardest part for her was hearing of friends who had been arrested, from her network and among close and extended family. "We still mourn them today. However, to our great satisfaction, all of the children we hid survived. Yet, for those children, the Liberation brought an end to a long period of waiting and hope. Unfortunately, most of these young people realized at the end of the war that they had lost one or both parents."

After the war, Liliane got married and had three sons. Today, she has seven grandchildren. "My three sons and my grandchildren all know this story well. One of them, who is studying filmmaking, even filmed me telling my life story." Liliane is the President of the Association of Hidden Children.

FRENCH HEROINES, 1940-1945
Interview with Liliane Klein-Lieber (July 22, 2002)

Interview with Yvette Bernard Farnoux
(June 12, 2003)

Yvette Bernard Farnoux[13], born Yvette Baumann, to a family of non-practicing Jews in Alsace, is an Auschwitz survivor. She has tried in vain to erase the serial number that remains tattooed on her forearm. She lives with her husband[14]. When I called her "Madame Farnoux," she clarified, "People usually call me Mrs. Bernard Farnoux. Jean-Guy Bernard was my first husband, a Resistance fighter who was deported and gassed."

In 1941, Yvette was a social worker in Lyon, at the *Commissariat au chômage*[15] headed by the famous Resistance fighter, Berty Albrecht. One day, Berty asked Yvette to bring food to eighteen young Resistance fighters imprisoned in Clermont-Ferrand. Yvette exclaimed, "Where do you expect me to find provisions?!" It was an era of wartime shortages and the Germans were deliberately starving the French. Nevertheless, Berty's motto was, as always, "'You'll manage.' I told her, 'I can't manage, even with the best intentions; I don't have a cent to buy food with!' She replied without hesitation, 'So steal some!' Thus, with a young colleague who worked for the Salvation Army, we ended up stealing food to help these eighteen captured young

---

[13] In *Les Femmes dans la Résistance en France* (Tallandier, 2003), the chapter entitled « Des femmes juives dans la Résistance » mentions Yvette Farnoux (pp. 209-210). She wrote her story in *Les Juifs dans la Résistance et la Libération. Histoire, témoignages, débats.* Texts gathered and presented by RHICOJ, Ed. Scribe, 1985 (pp. 104-108).
[14] Mr. Farnoux died in 2008.
[15] This Unemployment Office helped women who worked in workshops and would have been jobless were it not for this aid. "They were hired for jobs that paid no more than unemployment benefits." The organization was dependent upon the *Secours national*, which was created by Pétain and provided food for the poor.

Resistance fighters. That was how we procured twenty 2-pound jars of jam and everything edible in the offices of the *Secours National* that we were able to hide in an old cardboard suitcase." But as they waited on the platform of the Perrache train station in Lyon, the overstuffed suitcase popped open and—horror of horrors!—the jars of jams rolled all over the platform and even onto the train tracks! "I was sure we would be arrested for black-marketeering." Luckily, a few kindhearted souls helped them pick up the jars and put them back into the suitcase. "Then, as if by miracle, a gentleman arrived with some rope and helped me tie the suitcase shut so we could continue on our way. We always had to be prepared for the unexpected, which made it impossible for us to make arrangements ahead of time and even difficult to attempt anything at all." The precious stolen food was successfully delivered to the eighteen prisoners, thanks to the diligence of a few trustworthy guards.

"Finding provisions was the least of it," says Yvette, who also trained social workers. The biggest job was finding people in each *Département* of France who could take care of prisoners' families. "I had a vast network: national leaders found leaders in the *Départements*, who then found leaders in the cities. In some villages, people were in prison and our main job was to take care of their families: provide them with food—which was indeed a problem during the Occupation, reassure them, and deliver their letters." The social workers could also count on help from clergymen, "some of whom were extraordinary." There were lawyers who agreed to serve as intermediaries, and a few prison guards opened prison doors upon request. Many families did not know where the prisoners lived. "First we had to conduct an investigation to find out where they had been taken after their arrest. This was not always easy, since the Resistance fighters had false names and also because the phone was not a reliable means of communication. Any information could only be transmitted in person."

At just 23 years old, Yvette had subordinates who were much older than she was. "I had to earn the trust of the Resistance fighters' families, who were all afraid that I was coming to arrest them or that I was an emissary who would bring about their arrest."

While working at the *Commissariat au chômage*, Yvette was in charge of families of prisoners from the Resistance movement *Combat*. When Berty Albrecht was arrested in April 1942, Yvette replaced her as the Head of Social Services in this movement, which, in 1943, became known as the *Les Mouvements unis de Résistance* (United Resistance Movements, or *Murs*)[16] . They had to put together packages of provisions, which was difficult with the strict food rationing, and deliver them to the families. "That in itself was a lot of work." In addition, Yvette had to find Resistance fighters who were organizing parachute drops, in order to receive the money sent by the Americans or the British.

She even organized escapes, "which needed to be done very meticulously." A doctor informed her that drinking goat's milk could make one's temperature rise above 104°F. Yvette and her friends acquired the milk and passed it to the prisoners with the help of the guards. "I don't remember how we managed it, but we got the boys to drink that disgusting stuff." Those who drank the milk developed a high fever and were sent to the hospital, from which it was easier to escape. Doctors and nurses participated in the conspiracy.

---

[16]This movement was made up of three different ones: *Combat, Libération and Francs-Tireurs.*

Yvette was a young idealist and had no fear. As a Jew and a Resistance fighter, she knew, nevertheless, that she risked death. A young woman who worked with Yvette's husband and knew their address was arrested and buckled under torture, but not immediately. "Usually, when people cracked, they gave names very quickly, but she withstood three weeks of torture before she gave in. Her reasoning was that after three weeks, we would surely have disappeared."

"Would you tell me how you and your husband were arrested?" I asked hesitantly.

"It was a Sunday in January 1944. We had decided to spend a quiet Sunday. Neither one of us had any meetings. Around 7pm, we heard the doorbell. I was in the kitchen cooking mushrooms. It seems silly to remember that detail. Jean-Guy went to open the door. We were expecting my sister-in-law. When I came back to the living room, it was silent. Jean-Guy was sitting on a chair; his face was ashen and his hands were tied behind his back. A woman and a man were searching him. They found a gun on him and made us go down the stairs. I was eight and a half months pregnant. They were pushing me in the back. I thought it would be better if I fell and I let them push me, but I didn't fall. When we reached the bottom of the stairs, we thought we saw those infamous black cars [of the Gestapo]. But actually, they were hackney carriages. We were put into separate cabs and driven to the Gare d'Austerlitz, flanked by two Gestapo officers. We ended up in Orléans and Blois. It was beyond comprehension, like all of the absurdities of the time. I never saw Jean-Guy again."

"What about your child?" I asked.

FRENCH HEROINES, 1940-1945
Interview with Yvette Bernard Farnoux (June 12, 2003)

"I tried to kill myself[17] and almost succeeded. I gave birth to a stillborn baby. One of the first things the Gestapo woman told me was, 'We won't try to make you talk now, but you'll see, when the baby is born, if we torture it in front of you and in front of your husband, you will both tell us everything you know.' So I had no choice."

Yvette, with a wounded arm and weakened by the interrogations, torture and her failed suicide attempt, was transported to the hospital in Blois. From there, she escaped, but was caught. She spent a month in the Fresnes prison, which she found "almost pleasant" because, she explains, "Through the casement window, you could communicate quite well with the others." Then she spent three weeks at the Drancy transit camp before being sent to Auschwitz-Birkenau in April 1944.

At Auschwitz and Birkenau, the women's solidarity was key. At the end of January 1945, they tried to keep each other warm in the extreme cold. Then, Yvette was sent to Ravensbrück. "My job, along with many other women, was to transfer stones from a pile on the left to a pile on the right. A few days later, the stones in the right-side pile had to be transported to the left again. That was about as exciting as our work got. At one point, since the Germans saw that I had an incapacitated arm due to my suicide attempt, they gave me sewing to do. I did not know how to sew, so I took a pair of scissors and cut pieces of fabric into bits. I intentionally ruined everything they gave me to sew. It was probably pointless, but I thought that if everyone did that, it would be better than working for the Nazis."

---

[17]She had hidden a razor blade in the lining of her coat and used it to cut the veins of her left wrist.

One day, after the camp was liberated by the Soviet Union, a totally drunk American soldier showed up to tell the women he was coming to liberate them. Yvette wanted to go back to France. Behind the drunken soldier, there was another soldier in a U.S. uniform. It turned out that he was Mr. Farnoux, a Frenchman who had escaped from Grünwald. "We got married around 1946 and we had three children." The Farnoux now have nine grandchildren, to whom they never wanted to mention their wartime experiences. "We told our children, 'We have a few recordings which you will watch after we die.' I don't want them to feel sorry for us."

After the war, Yvette and her second husband could no longer stand being in Paris. "The Parisian frivolity was intolerable to us, and a lot of our friends were gone." They moved to Dakar, where the French Post Office and Telecommunications Network (PTT) was happy to rehire Mr. Farnoux, their former employee. The Farnoux stayed in Senegal for three years, then came back to Paris for a little while before leaving again for Morocco. Five years later, they moved to Algeria. Those were the dark years. Yvette says sadly, "I felt like I was reliving the same thing. And this time, it was the French instead of the Germans."

Interview with Huguette Prety (June 22, 2002)

In 1940, Huguette Prety was 18 years old. Her parents owned a clothing shop in Paris, on *rue Cler*, a busy shopping street. At the beginning of the Occupation, the shop window displayed a sign in German, *"judisches geschaft,"* "Jewish business." Huguette had a bad premonition. "Jews did not always have a sense of reality and the impending danger." She begged her parents to leave Paris, but her father wanted to stay for a little while longer. Nevertheless, "he did appoint a friend, who was president of the clothing retailers' union, as provisional manager." Thus, with her 8-year-old brother, 13-year-old sister and their mother, Huguette left the occupied zone for the so-called "free zone."[18]

She chose to travel on December 31, 1940, in hopes that the Germans would be busy celebrating the New Year. They went to Avignon, to the house of an aunt whose husband was not Jewish. A WWI veteran, this non-Jewish uncle worked in the City Hall, in the food ration card department. Both the aunt and uncle then left for Brives, near Limoges, taking Huguette's family with them.

Huguette started working at the Brives hospital, under the protection of the nuns who ran it. She took classes at the Red Cross. The family lived near the hospital, where Huguette spent the night when "things were very bad and she was in danger of being arrested." In late 1941, she was studying for the Red Cross exam. At the time, she wrote in her diary, "Why worry so much about ending up in a concentration camp?" Like many others, she had no idea what was going on in the camps. She thought they were labor camps. She now thinks that the political leaders of the

[18]The south of France became an occupied zone after November 11, 1942.

time must have known. "Churchill or the others could have bombed the railways leading to the concentration camps. Yet, nothing of the sort was done by the Allies to stop the mass deportation of French Jews."

In the free zone, Jews did not wear yellow stars, but after a while, in Brives, the stamp "Jew" became mandatory on identity cards.

Huguette was in luck: her classmate and friend, Eliane Barre, came to visit her and "she gave me her identity and her mother gave hers to my mother." Huguette was relieved to be able to acquire Eliane's birth certificate at the Chavagnac city hall, with a date of birth and a stamp. With this document in hand, she rushed to buy a blank identity card to which she attached her photograph. She could now abandon her Jewish last name, "Goldenberg," and be known henceforth as Eliane Barre.

In 1943, her parents moved to Toulouse, to the house of some non-Jewish former suppliers of their store. "I found out later that my parents were not really welcome, because their arrival complicated things." Huguette was living at the hospital and running the phthisiology[19] department. She remained undisturbed, although many people knew her true identity. She decided to move to Neris-les-bains, in the Allier *Département*, with an aunt who was not declared as a Jew. Huguette cannot say exactly why she moved there, "but it gave me a place to go."

She went to live in a hotel under her false name. She did not properly falsify her Red Cross diploma as Eliane Barre, but nobody seemed to take any notice. She applied for a job at the hospital of Montluçon, only to be rejected. Perhaps her identity seemed suspicious? Shortly afterwards, the spa hospital

---

[19]Branch of medicine studying tuberculosis.

of Neris-les-bains was transformed into a military hospital and Huguette was hired there.

Meanwhile, the *Maquis* (Guerilla movement) was in need of medicine. She found out about this, but could not say anything. No one knew she was Jewish. Later, the *Maquis* came to the hospital because they needed a nurse. "Naturally, I followed them." In the *Maquis*, she was known by two names: Eliane Barre and Second Lieutenant Marianne.

The Maquis movement she worked for was located in the middle of the Tronçet forest. "The *Maquisards* had taken over an old people's home. They had found farming families who took in the elderly inhabitants and had the entire house to use as a hospital." They held German prisoners and wounded captive SS women. "I worked there until the Liberation. I cannot for the life of me remember why I did not return to Paris immediately. I found a document from back then stating, 'Eliane Barre of the social service is authorized to circulate day and night in the Toulouse region as her job requires.' It was signed by the proxy head of the intelligence service, a deputy, Captain Bouteville."

On December 23, 1944, she received an order to go to St. Girons to distribute Christmas care packages to soldiers patrolling the border. "That had nothing to do with the Resistance Movement," she notes.

Having traveled to Foix and Toulouse several times with the F.F.I., she went back to Paris after the Libération. She got married in 1948 and now has two daughters, nine grandchildren and two great-grandchildren.

At the end of our interview, Huguette showed me a small, front-wheel-drive Citroën similar to those used by the SS, but labeled "F.F.I." She told me, "I drove into the *Maquis* wilderness in this type of car. I had my Red Cross arm band, which I dangled out the car window to make people think I was with the Red Cross, so that they would not shoot at me."

Interview with Andrée Warlin (June 17, 2002).

Andrée Warlin[20] was born in 1914 in Switzerland. Her parents were French Jews. In 1936, she married a Parisian gynecologist. In September 1939, the "Phony War" began. Dr. Warlin was mobilized as an army doctor Captain. Andrée was eight months pregnant. "I was miserable, both financially and morally," she told me.

In May 1940, the German army swept through Europe. Andrée, along with thousands of other French people, suddenly found herself on the run with her mother-in-law and the baby. She had no news of her husband until the end of June, when he was demobilized and they were reunited in the Gers region. With heavy hearts, they left their baby son with Andrée's parents in Basel, where he would be safe.

In September 1940, the doctor returned to his job at the Tarnier hospital. In the summer of 1942, his colleagues warned him that there were rumors of an upcoming roundup of all French Jews in prominent positions: doctors, lawyers and other professionals. "They did not distinguish between foreigners and French citizens in these roundups."

The Warlins had to flee once again. They moved to Lyon, where they became involved with the Resistance movement. They worked for the Second Bureau, an intelligence agency. They were full of apprehension and wanted to travel through Switzerland to join General de Gaulle in Great Britain. At the end

---

[20]She published her memoirs, entitled *L'impossible oubli*, Pensée Universelle, 1980. Mrs. Warlin recently showed me a text she published in the journal, *Bulletin des Amitiés de la Résistance*, (June 17th, 2005), entitled, "Crimes contre l'humanité. C'était hier : De Fresnes à Drancy." ("Crimes against humanity. It was yesterday: From Fresnes to Drancy.")

of December 1942, the left for Annemasse with some friends. They carried with them information on enemy divisions to pass along to the English Consul in Basel. The Gestapo arrested them at the Swiss border. Had they been followed? "No matter what happens, I will never feel more dread than I felt at that moment. It was unbearable." Andrée's husband had just enough time to swallow the photo that would allow them to recognize their network leader.

They were put in a car, escorted by the Gestapo army, to Annemasse, where they were interrogated separately. They undressed Andrée and discovered maps of Hermann Goehring's[21] factory. Insults rained down on her: "Dirty whore! Bitch! Spy!" They brought in a huge dog, which did not frighten Andrée. She lost all self-control, yelling, "You are cruel monsters! You are no longer human." Then, she told me, "Two drunkards in Nazi uniforms were called to the rescue. They held a revolver to my neck." She was sure that she and her husband would be shot for being French, Jewish[22] and "terrorists." "I instinctively recited the Sh'ma Israël."

They were sent to the Hotel Terminus in Lyon, then transferred to the prison in Châlons-sur-Saône. There were six people per cell and it was very cold. There was no running water, no beds and no heating. "We had to wash in the courtyard in front of the soldiers." One freezing, dismal morning in December 1942, she was awakened at 5a.m. She saw her husband but they did not have a chance to talk. Other Resistance fighters joined them in this

---

[21]Minister of Aviation and Commander of the Luftwaffe (Air Force) (1935), Head of the Wartime Economy (1940), he made a fortune from artwork stolen by the Nazis. Due to his many failures as head of the Luftwaffe, Hitler expelled him from the party in 1945. Sentenced to death by the Nuremberg tribunal, he poisoned himself.

[22]At the time, their last name was Weill, which they later changed to Warlin.

convoy, all chained together. They left Châlons for Paris and arrived at the Gare de Lyon at lunchtime. Andrée asked the guard for permission to buy some food for herself and her companions in misfortune. Accompanied by her jailer, she begged to receive some bread without tickets. "Ask your friend, he must have some," she was told. Andrée clarified, "I'm not his friend; I'm his prisoner, along with the others over there." Immediately, the customers present all stood up and gathered the little money and tickets they had to give to her. She bought sandwiches. "That gave me courage, because I realized there were still kind people out there." She joined the prisoners and they were locked in the prison van.

Dr. Warlin and his wife thought they were together for the last time in the tiny cell of the "salad basket."[23] Suddenly, a French policeman bellowed, "Are there any Jews among you?" All the anxious voices replied in the negative, except for the Warlins. "We are Jews," they said with shocking boldness. "The guard came close to our cell and said quietly, "Hang in there; it is almost over. They are in front of Smolensk and Stalingrad and no longer advancing." Unfortunately, this did not change the situation for Andrée and her husband.

Andrée was incarcerated in the Fresnes prison for six long months. One morning at dawn, she heard the guard's footsteps stopping in front of some cells. It was a blood-chilling sound, as it could mean trial, deportation or death. "As a Resistance fighter and a Jew, I knew I had no chance of survival." She had no news of her husband, she was covered with boils and suffering from

---

[23]The police car was called a "panier à salade" (salad basket) because it held witnesses and suspects mixed together and shaken up by bumps on the road like salad in a salad spinner.

hunger. "In the morning, through a hole in the armored door, they handed us a bowl of revolting murky liquid they called coffee and a lump of moldy bread."

After three weeks, Andrée was allowed to send out her dirty laundry for cleaning. She thought of her sister, the only person who might have thought to look for her. "Indeed, two weeks later, my laundry was returned to me without comment. I knew that if my sister had sent it, she would have found a way to let me know. I scrutinized the clothes, and found a message sewn in pink thread on a pink bra. My 'little' sister had jeopardized her safety to give me a sign of life. How could I send a reply? We were not supposed to have access to needles or thread, but our jailer could not resist the pleasure of having her stockings mended for free or having us knit sweaters and jackets for her. Thus, I obtained a needle and thread so my sister and I were able to continue our correspondence."

With a corset busk, she pierced a small hole in the opaque glass of her cell window to communicate with other prisoners, and covered it up with a photo of her baby. The days dragged by. In the winter, nightfall came early, and despite the meager supply of books she was able to borrow, the days in Fresnes were full of anguish and gloom, and "hunger gnawed at us." Every morning, Andrée heard doors being unlocked. Prisoners were sent to the shooting squad. "The Marseillaise sounded, then there was silence and jailers' yells."

"One day," says Andrée, "I discovered body lice in my so-called 'mattress.' I caught one and put it in a small bottle to prove to the jailer that I wasn't making up stories. I was subjected to the shower and brutal disinfection."

Six months later, Andrée was released from her cell. She was taken to a hallway on the first floor. "For the first time, I saw only

FRENCH HEROINES, 1940-1945
Interview with Andrée Warlin (June 17, 2002).

people wearing a yellow star sewn onto their clothing. All these Jewish prisoners were crowded into this sordid place, women on one side and men on the other." The Jews' fate was clear: they were to die. The women, including Andrée, were taken by police van to the "Depot." She and the other starving women turned to some nuns, who refused to sell them sandwiches. However, the poor girls known as "fallen women" mustered up the money to buy them some bread.

In June 1943, the Warlins were taken to the camp at Drancy. The open air invigorated them, but the camp was an appalling sight. Three towers marked the unfinished buildings. From afar, the Warlins could see a throng of idle people swarming in the courtyard: priests and nuns, "friends" of the Jews, Resistance fighters or Jewish men, women, children and old people. Lawyers and doctors mingled with beggars; actors and academics were sweeping the courtyard. They all faced the same degrading plight. "We were reduced to 'just Jews,' like all the others." Dr. Warlin continued his work as a doctor, delivering babies who were to be deported the next day.

In July 1943, the camp was handed over from the French police to the Germans. New interrogations were conducted. Everyone was subject to deportation, except those who could prove they were 100% Aryan.

One day, Andrée was sent to work outside the camp. Drancy prisoners had to move everything out of a Jewish apartment[24]. "I used that semi-liberty to contact my sister, and under the pretext

---

[24]In their book, *Des camps dans Paris. Austerlitz, Lévitan, Bassano. Juillet 1943-août 1944* (Fayard, 2003), Jean-Marc Dreyfus and Sarah Gensburger provide a good description of the work that half-Jews or Jews married to non-Jews were forced to do in these camps that were little known at the time. They unloaded and sorted items stolen from the Jews.

of going to buy sandwiches, I had lunch with her in a restaurant. I got my hands on some Freemason files I found in the Jews' apartment, and when we got back to the camp, I destroyed them."

Dr. Warlin was working with one of two teams of prisoners to build an escape tunnel. "The work, done at night, required superhuman strength. They needed to bring in oxygen, haul out the stones, all without being seen by the jailers." The tunnel was almost finished when a former prisoner of the camp, transferred elsewhere, unmaliciously and naively boasted about the original invention. They were denounced, but luckily, Dr. Warlin was spared, as only one of the tunnel-digging teams was accused. The guilty ones were punished, deprived of food, and locked in solitary confinement until they were deported. Along with some other prisoners, Andrée and her husband covertly brought them food.

The cruelty of the torturers running the camp was beyond words. "One day, they forced a father to whip his son with a strip of leather in front of all the other prisoners. When he did not hit hard enough, the torturers took over."

In the camp, Andrée noticed a six-year-old girl and her 15-year-old sister, whose last name, "Amon," was not known in Germany. She decided to save them. "If you can muster the courage," she told the teen-age girl, "tell them you are not Jewish. I will get you a Baptism certificate." Andrée's sister, who worked for the Resistance movement, acquired the Baptism certificates from a priest, Abbé Menardais ("honored as 'Righteous among the Nations' after the war"). Jacqueline Amon was brave enough to stand up to Brunner, who accepted the false Baptism certificate. Jacqueline and her little sister avoided the last deportation.

FRENCH HEROINES, 1940-1945
Interview with Andrée Warlin (June 17, 2002).

Andrée and her husband were about to be deported, but Dr. Warlin fell ill. The camp physician told the Germans, "He has diphtheria; he will infect everyone." Andrée adds, "It was the only time a prisoner was able to avoid deportation thanks to a contagious disease."

"We saw buses arrive, filled with children ages two to sixteen. They had been collected at orphanages. The Germans' van was in the courtyard. It was equipped with a radio. Risking his life, a prisoner turned on the radio on June 6, 1944 and heard that the Allies had landed on the coast of Normandy. The news spread like gunpowder. For the first time since the war started, we had a glimmer of hope. The days passed. We sensed that our cruel overseers were getting nervous, and thus more dangerous. They organized new deportations. They did not care that German trains were scarce. The main thing was to kill a maximum of Jews."

The German guards were panic-stricken, and admitted they must leave, but promised to be "more lenient" when they returned. The prisoners hid compromising files under Andrée's bed, in anticipation of liberty. The rumors were reassuring: the Allies were advancing and the Germans were being forced to flee.

Andrée had witnessed the arrival of young, enthusiastic Nazis and now, from the unfinished buildings of the Drancy camp, she was watching them retreat, "a poor old bunch in place of a sacrificed generation of young Nazis. They were leaving, dressed in hooded capes that were too long or too short."

One day, Andrée was sweeping the courtyard when she saw her sister Madeleine outside the barbed wires. Madeleine, risking arrest, was signaling to her that there was a parcel labeled "Ratisbonne"[25] hidden under the piano. The package contained

---

[25]A city in Germany whose name was used as a code by Andrée and her sister.

weapons, but they were never to be used. On August 19, 1944, Nordling, the Swedish Consul, arrived at the camp and announced to the prisoners that they were free. Andrée's sister came in a German car to pick up the weapons that she had stolen and distributed them to the Resistance fighters.

Volunteers stayed at the camp and with Nordling's help, made ID cards and distributed small amounts of money to the poor people who had nowhere to go. "After two days, a Red Cross ambulance took us to the center of Paris," says Andrée. They went to Dr. Warlin's grandmother's house in the 14th *arrondissement*.

It was the beginning of the Liberation. "Paris was at war and everyone was behind the 'barricades' against the collaborators. The Warlins finally returned home to the avenue Marceau. Their apartment had just been abandoned. "The chamber pots had not been emptied. Photos of Hitler and Himmler hung on the walls. The apartment had been used as a *Kommandantur* (headquarters). Yet, Paris had not yet been liberated." There was fighting going on in the capital. The streets were stripped of cobblestones and the Resistants defended the city against what remained of the Nazis, Milicia and traitors. It was a bloody battle. Young people were dying on street corners. "On the radio, we heard cries for help from the *Mairies* (city halls) of the *arrondissements*, 'Send weapons to the Mairie of the 6th *arrondissement*, Send weapons to the Mairie of the 11th,' and all of a sudden, we heard all the bells of *Notre Dame* begin to ring. It was incredible. Paris had been liberated." Leclerc's army, along with the Allies, had entered Paris.

Andrée and her husband were reunited with their little boy in the summer of 1945.

Interview with Marthe Cohn (August 8, 2002)

Marthe, a charming Frenchwoman born in Metz to a devout Jewish family, now lives with her American husband in a suburb of Los Angeles. She holds the distinction of being the only woman interviewed for this book who worked as a spy in the French army.

In 1939, Marthe and her family left Metz[26] for Poitiers, southwest of Paris. After the armistice that Maréchal Pétain signed with Germany in 1940, the Germans and the Vichy regime promulgated a series of anti-Jewish laws[27]. In Poitiers, near the line of demarcation, Marthe's family, the Hoffnungs, befriended a family of farmers whose land was on the border between occupied and free France. "Almost every day, strangers rang our doorbell to ask for help."

In Poitiers, Marthe worked as an interpreter at the town hall, in the *Bureau des Réquisitions*[28] established by the Germans. She lost her job when Jews were banned from the public service. One of her former colleagues from the town hall offered valuable assistance: "Monsieur Charpentier approached me on the street

---

[26]Metz is in eastern France, near the Franco-German border; it was German territory for 50 years up to WWI. [Translator's note]

[27]On September 27, 1940, there was a census of Jews in the occupied zone. In October 1940, Jews had to register at the town hall and have the word "Jew" stamped on their identity papers. On October 3, the first "Statute on Jews" was passed (see footnote 4 p. 29, interview with Liliane Klein-Lieber). On June 2, 1941, the second "Statute on Jews" banned Jews from practicing a long list of professions. On May 29, 1942, it became mandatory for all Jews over the age of 6 to wear a yellow star. On July 8, 1942, in the occupied zone, Jews were banned from theaters, restaurants and public gardens. They could only buy provisions between 3 and 4 p.m.

[28]Marthe did not like working there because the Bureau was "designed specifically to facilitate the systematic theft of anything French by the occupying forces" (*Behind Enemy Lines,* p. 62 (42-Harmony Books)), but at least she was making money.

and offered to provide my family and me with forged documents without the Jewish stamp. It was an unbelievable stroke of luck. This man was saving our lives while risking his own and that of his loved ones. When I offered to compensate him for this service, he began to cry and I was so ashamed! His offer was motivated by duty and compassion, and thanks to him we were later able to leave Poitiers and survive the Occupation."

On October 6th, 1941, Marthe enrolled at the Red Cross nursing college in Poitiers, but she had to cut her studies short because her family was no longer safe. She was able to finish her studies in 1943 in Marseille.

In June 1942, Marthe's younger sister Stéphanie was arrested for helping the Resistance. To help her sister escape, Marthe organized a crossing of the Line of Demarcation for seven members of her family. She was helped by her fiancé, Jacques Delaunay, several classmates, and some neighbors, including a priest. "Since my grandmother could barely walk, we seated her on my bicycle. My mother supported her on the seat while I pushed the steering wheel." Stéphanie, who had helped so many people cross the border, refused to flee for fear of jeopardizing her family's safety. Interrogated by the Gestapo, she did not want to name her accomplices, spent a month in prison and was then sent to the internment camps in Drancy and Pithiviers. She was deported to Auschwitz on the day of Yom Kippur (Day of Atonement) in September 1942, never to be seen again.

In November 1943, Marthe, now a registered nurse, went to live with her sister Cécile in Paris, where they changed apartments frequently to avoid being arrested. An agency found her a job nursing an elderly woman at home, since working in a hospital would have been much too risky.

In August 1944, Paris was liberated and Marthe decided to join the French army to continue to fight.

In November 1944, she was sent to Alsace to join a group of Resistance fighters who had fought in Paris. The group was headed by Colonel Fabien, a 26-year-old Communist. "He was famous for having been the first Resistance fighter to kill a German, in 1943 in the Paris metro. He and his group of 700 men made a crucial contribution to the city's liberation." The army, wary of former collaborators trying to gain credibility, and seeing how young and inexperienced she was, did not make things easy for her. She did end up achieving her goal, but her military career was off to a bad start. She was mocked by an officer who thought she was unworthy of the army and wanted to send her home. Furious, she retorted, "Army Command assigned me to your unit and whether you like it or not, I intend to stay."

As a nurse, Marthe should have been ranked as an officer, but she was downgraded to a sergeant. Her job title, she was told, was "social worker." "I had no idea what was expected of me." She went to see the soldiers on the front line, helped them write letters to their parents and friends and did her best to procure the supplies they lacked.

Three weeks later, in the village where the regiment was quartered, she ran into Colonel Fabien. He was going on his lunch break. "Would you be kind enough to answer my phone for me while I am out?" he asked. "I could not possibly have said no to a Colonel, "Marthe says with a laugh. He apologized for having nothing for her to read as all the books were in German. She replied that she spoke fluent German. The Colonel, astonished, stared at her wide-eyed and then asked if she would be willing to do intelligence work. She accepted without hesitation. "Once he was out the door, I suddenly doubted my decision, remembering the line from Molière's play, *The Trickeries of Scapin*, 'Mais que Diable, vas-tu faire dans cette galère' ('How in the name of the devil will you get out of that mess?')"

A few days later, she was taken to Mulhouse. "Lieutenants Latour and Vérin were in charge of my training. I learned to read a map, shoot small pistols and machine guns, recognize different uniforms, officers' ranks and units. I trained my memory to retain anything that could be of interest: places, meetings, documents, etc. Then I was taught to code the information." After ten days of intensive training, Lieutenant Vérin interrogated her to test her reflexes. She passed the test, so he drove her in a jeep to Cernay in the Vosges Mountains, where she joined the Commandos d'Afrique, a regiment of the First French Army. It was snowing and freezing cold. They had to drive the jeep with the headlights off because they were so close to the front line. "For my first mission that January of 1945, I had to wear civilian clothing, which was not nearly warm enough. To top it all off, I only had a little suitcase with a change of clothes."

They arrived at the Saint-André psychiatric hospital and descended to the basement, using matches for light. They found Major Rigaud, sound asleep. Vérin shook him awake, introduced him to Mademoiselle Lenôtre (Marthe's code name in the army). Rigaud grumbled, "Welcome. Find somewhere to sit," and promptly went back to sleep. "I had caught a bad cold; I was coughing my lungs out and I was very tired." In the darkness, Marthe slid off of her chair, her teeth chattering, and her stretched-out legs felt a mattress with someone on it. She lay with her head near the sleeping person's feet. She gradually pulled his cover over herself and in the morning, her "mattress-mate" awoke with a start as his hand accidentally touched her stockinged legs, "'*Nom de Dieu, une femme!*' Once the initial shock had passed, he took off my shoes and massaged my feet and legs, saving me from frostbite."

The next day, she met Colonel Bouvet, the commanding officer of the Commandos d'Afrique, who immediately employed her in headquarters. "My first task was interrogating Alsatian civilians and POWs recently captured after German troops had begun to retreat. I was lucky enough to obtain important information on the positions of German troops who were still fighting relentlessly in Alsace."

A few days later, Bouvet ordered her to infiltrate enemy lines. She had to cross a valley to reach the Amselkopf. "I was 24 years old. Dressed in civilian clothing, I left Thann with a heavily armed military escort. We walked four miles through the snowy mountains. It was early January or late February 1945. We walked for hours in total silence." Then her escort turned back, leaving her to carry on alone. Carrying a map was not an option, so she had memorized her route. If stopped, she had to say her name was Martha Ulrich. She was a nurse who had lost her parents in a bombing; she hated the Allies, and her fiancé Hans, whose photograph and letters she carried, had disappeared. Hans was an actual prisoner of war in France, whom the secret services had forced to provide the photograph and letters.

Unfortunately, the guide misdirected Marthe, so she went the wrong way and her mission failed. Instead of German soldiers, she ended up face to face with Moroccan soldiers of the First French Army. They mistook her for a German spy, insulted her and threatened to shoot her. Later, she was summoned by Captain Mollat, who refused to admit the guide's mistake and accused

Marthe of having taken the wrong path on her own or being too afraid to complete her mission. Marthe defended herself and proved the error had not been hers.

On April 11, 1945, a secret agent named Georges Lemaire drives her to Schaffhausen, an enclave of Switzerland that jutted into Germany, for a new mission. Having crossed the border, she would go to Freiburg-en-Brisgau and contact the German friends of Dr. Mueller, an Alsatian doctor with whom she had supposedly worked as a nurse in the city of Konstanz. Dr. Mueller had actually escaped from Germany after the liberation of Alsace and returned home to that region.

Neutral Switzerland was divided from Nazi Germany by a narrow road that was patrolled by two soldiers whose paths crossed at regular intervals as they switched positions. From her hiding place in the woods on the Swiss side, Marthe had to cross the road at the moment the border guards had their backs turned. Lemaire had promised to protect her in case things went awry.

"I knew full well that I could not count on his interference, which would have caused an international incident. Holding my little suitcase, I crawled towards the bush closest to the place where the guards passed each other. Frozen in fear, I waited a whole hour watching them come and go, unable to propel myself forward. Finally, I grabbed my suitcase and got up. Walking in a trance towards the city of Singen, as expected, I came face to face with the guard walking in my direction. I raised my arm and saluted him casually with a 'Heil Hitler.' He checked my papers and asked me where I was going. 'To Singen to visit some friends,' I replied. He gave me back my papers and I left quickly. After this intensely stressful moment, I was suddenly filled with euphoria and immense pride for having overcome my fear."

In Singen, Ilse, a young woman living with her father and her baby, provided her with food and a bed for the night. "I had told her Dr. Mueller sent me, and his name worked wonders. I was welcomed with open arms." The next morning, Ilse noticed Marthe's torn stockings and became suspicious. "How do I know you are not a spy?" she asked Marthe, who burst out laughing and replied, "Look at me, Frau Schmidt! Do I look like a spy?" "No, not really," replied Ilse in embarrassment. Marthe proceeded to tell her about her lost fiancé, and the story struck a chord, as her hostess's husband was fighting on the Russian front. "She was touched by my desperate efforts to find Hans and by the photos and letters from my 'fiancé' that I showed her." Ilse then took her to the train station, where Marthe reserved a ticket for Freiburg for the following night. (Trains did not run in the daytime due to constant Allied bombings.)

In Freiburg, Marthe went to stay with Gertrude Schröder, who welcomed her warmly at the mention of Dr. Mueller's name. But one afternoon, a friend of Gertrude's came to visit and asked Marthe the name of the clinic where she had supposedly worked in Konstanz. "Caught off guard, I said 'Bodensee Clinic' without thinking. Staring at me, Gertrude Schröder's friend said, 'That sounds more like a hotel or a restaurant.' Unwilling to back down, I quickly replied, 'Indeed, it was a hotel that was transformed into a clinic during the war.'"

Marthe's assignment was to contact an Alsatian, Dr. Schaeffer, who had married a German woman before 1939. She had to give him a letter from his parents in which they begged him to come back to France. Marthe went to see him and revealed to him that she was in the French intelligence and asked him to help her. "Far from showing gratitude, he became enraged, screaming that his wife was German and that it was outrageous of me to ask him such a thing. How dare I ask him to betray his adopted country?!" Shocked, Marthe tried to calm him down and refused to give him her address for fear that he would turn her in to the authorities. She made up an excuse and fled quickly. She took a very long route, constantly looking over her shoulder to make sure she was not being followed before returning to Gertrude's house.

Later, French POWs working on farms provided Marthe with valuable information on troops around Freiburg. She met two Alsatian women who had been forcibly enlisted into the German army and who missed their homes and families. They informed her about the battalion stationed in Freiburg "in exchange for my promise to facilitate their return to France." With these and other contacts, Marthe was able to set up an active network. From Freiburg, she went to a village further north to see Dr. Grunwald, a friend of Captain Ligouzat, head of the Intelligence Service in the Commandos d'Afrique. Dr. Grunwald lived near the Siegfried Line, also known as the Westwall, a series of fortifications along Germany's western border.

On the way, Marthe joined a group of women and a noncommissioned SS officer, Sergeant Major Helmut Werner, who had been wounded on the Russian front. Werner kept bragging about the number of Poles, Russians and Jews he had killed. "He gave us a thorough account of the atrocities he and his fellow soldiers had committed, without sparing any details. The women were laughing, congratulating him and showing unreserved approval of the horrors he had committed. As we walked side by side, he announced to me that he could smell a Jew from a mile away! Then all of a sudden, his chatter abruptly ceased…" Helmut Werner had fainted.

"Thrilled at the opportunity to gain favor with the group, I took on my role as a nurse to bring the executioner back to his senses. The Nazi recovered and pledged eternal gratitude to me. He extended a warm invitation to visit him at the Westwall." Marthe's next stop was the farm of an anti-Nazi family near the Swiss border to pass on the information she had collected back to her antenna. She then returned to Freiburg. "Gertrude and her fiancé, who were kind enough to put me up once more, talked only of the imminent arrival of the French troops. They had just heard the news on the local radio."

She left immediately and walked for two hours to reach the Westwall, where she tried to find the sadistic soldier she had helped when he fainted, Helmut Werner. However, she found the place empty. Two soldiers told her that everyone had deserted the Siegfried Line. She rushed back to Freiburg. Along the way, she ran into a group of German soldiers whose orders were to defend the city. "I told them how much I admired their courage, and then I announced weepingly that all the troops had deserted the Westwall. I exhorted them to defend us valiantly. I told them, 'You are the only ones standing between the French army and the rest of Germany. You are our last hope!' Then I continued on my way, and when I turned around I saw them all drop their weapons and run away."

In Freiburg, everyone had gone into hiding. Alone on the main boulevard, Marthe saw a French tank advancing towards her. She stopped it, raising her hand and spreading her fingers in a V for victory. She was taken in the tank to see Major Petit of the Second Zouave Battalion. At first he did not believe that she was truly a First Army secret agent, so he verified her identity. Satisfied (and impressed) by the confirmation he received from her antenna, he extended an invitation for dinner and lodging for the night at headquarters. The next morning, he offered to help her return to her antenna in France, but she refused, telling him, "The south has not yet been won and my mission is far from finished. If you want to help me, please find me a bicycle." She left headquarters and recrossed the front south of Freiburg by bicycle.

"I was often very frightened, but most of the time the extreme tension helped me overcome the cold, hunger, exhaustion, fear and danger. I begged all the German soldiers I met to defend 'our' country against the French army that had invaded Freiburg with cannons, columns of tanks and troops made up mostly of sinister-faced Arab and black soldiers." To win the Germans' trust, she used the photos and letters of her alleged fiancé, Hans.

In the evening, exhausted and starving, she stopped in an empty restaurant. The owner wore a Nazi party pin on his lapel. He looked at her suspiciously and told his wife that this girl was not to be trusted. Marthe overheard him. "I was terrified, my teeth were chattering and I thought of running away, but I stayed seated, knowing that if I ran, I would quickly be caught." She ordered soup. The restaurateur brought it and sat down in front of her. "I suddenly found myself perfectly in control, the absolute calm that came in moments of grave danger." Marthe explained to him that she had come from Freiburg and that her parents had been killed in an allied bombing. Once again, she took out the photos and letters of her lost "fiancé" and, with a tear-filled voice, described her vain efforts to find the love of her life. Moved by her sad story, the man was convinced his lovelorn customer was telling the truth. "He informed me that a convoy of German soldiers was moving south, and took me to the road they were on. He helped lift me and my bicycle onto the back of a horse-drawn pig wagon."

Marthe must have developed a sixth sense during the Occupation. She stopped in a small town on her way back to Freiburg, and decided to stay there for the night. An old man she ran into confirmed the wisdom of her decision, as he himself had run into a military checkpoint on the outskirts of the town and had been detained for hours as they checked his papers. He suggested she spend the night at the home of two kind sisters of his acquaintance. Marthe thanked him warmly and took his advice.

Two days later, she arrived at the farm. Greta, one of the farmer's daughters, was married to an Alsatian who worked for Marthe's antenna. His task was to take the letter Marthe gave Greta to his superior officers. Unfortunately, when Marthe arrived, he had just left. She had some information to pass on immediately: while walking through the mountains, she had seen a huge military camp in a valley below. A few days later, she had run into an officer who had believed her sob story about her fiancé and had entrusted her with the whereabouts in the Black Forest of what remained of the German army. "Naturally, it was vital that I transmit this information as quickly as possible. I had no choice but to transmit my message to the Basel intelligence service through a Swiss customs officer, according to the directions I had been given. I quickly wrote a long letter without taking the time to code it. At dawn, Greta, her sister and I left the farm."

Greta explained to Marthe where the Swiss and French customs houses were, on the other side of the barbed wire. About to knock on the window of the building she thought was the Swiss customs house, Marthe saw a portrait of Hitler staring at her from the wall. Greta had confused her right and her left! "Once again, I was insanely lucky," Marthe said. "The Germans were sleeping." She ran away and saw the Swiss soldier on the other side waving to her desperately from behind a tree. She ran to him and gave him the letter, telling him she was a secret agent. "This letter, I told him, must be delivered before 11a.m. to Colonel Reinhart in Basel. The customs officer, certain that I wanted to stay in Switzerland, offered me an escort to where I wanted to go, but I refused. To my great surprise, this towering giant of a man clicked his heels together and saluted me. I returned his salute and left." Back at the farm, she met Gunther, Greta's older brother, who gave her important information on his unit, which was based in the region. As he was showing her their exact location on a map, a neighbor, whose husband was fighting at the Russian front, entered without knocking. She obviously did not believe the explanation they gave her. "Convinced that she would alert the authorities, my friends made me leave quickly."

Marthe hopped on her bike and headed east. Near the small town of Waldshut, she stopped in front of a property swarming with agitated soldiers and moving vehicles. She came closer and played her role of damsel in distress looking for her lost love. "Having listened to my story, the sentinel, who had luckily never seen Hans, told me that his division had been forced back by enemy forces and was planning to cross the border that very evening and surrender to the Swiss authorities in order to avoid falling into French hands."

A French column was advancing towards them from Freiburg and white sheets of surrender hung from every window. In the town square, a group of frightened Germans pointed to a French jeep that had just appeared. Taking her only chance, Marthe dashed towards the jeep on her bike as the Germans screamed insults at her back.

FRENCH HEROINES, 1940-1945
Interview with Marthe Cohn (August 8, 2002)

"I cried breathlessly, 'Take me to your headquarters immediately! I have vital information for your commanding officer.'" As she climbed into the jeep next to the officer, Marthe recognized the insignia on his sleeve. "Are you with the Second Zouaves?" she asked. He said yes, and she asked him to take her to Major Petit. "I gave him all the information I had collected. When the general received the information, he did not react immediately, but ended up giving the order to attack the German division near Waldshut. Several French soldiers lost their lives in the skirmish, but during the night, the Germans surrendered to the Swiss, who promptly handed them over to the French."

Marthe remained with the Second Zouave Battalion. She took inventories of factories and businesses for the French army and tried to reclaim goods stolen from France. On May 8, 1945, the French regiment received an order to occupy a northern Rhineland sector. Major Petit handed Marthe the keys to a brand new beige-colored BMW requisitioned by the army. She did not know how to drive, but orders were orders, and she took a one-hour crash course. She stayed in Rhineland for several more weeks with the Second Zouaves, and then, upon orders from Captain Zimmerman, she joined her antenna in Konstanz. "A short time afterwards, I was transferred to an antenna near Lindau in Bavaria, on the Austrian border. My new commanding officer assigned me to the Military Government of Lindau, where I was in charge of the office of travel passes. No Bavarian German could travel or have family or friends visit without my authorization. Unofficially, I recruited Germans who were willing to give us information on sectors controlled by our Allies in exchange for travel passes."

Marthe stayed in Lindau from July 1945 to January 1946. Then she volunteered for the French Far East Expeditionary Force. In February 1946, she returned to Marseille and boarded a boat for Indochina, where she worked as a nurse for three years. "My work in the secret service was now behind me." In 1952, her sister Cécile and her husband invited her to live with them in Geneva. She lived with them for a year and studied at Cantonal Hospital, and then she met her future husband, Major Lloyd Cohn, a medical student. In 1956, she immigrated with him to the U.S., where they got married in 1958.

Today, at age 86, the indomitable Marthe is more active than ever. She gives lectures at schools[29], museums and synagogues and is a guest of honor of many associations.

---

[29]Since she lives near Pomona College where I teach, we meet every year when she comes to speak to my students. They are always fascinated by her accounts and some of them have even contributed to spreading her fame. I discovered with surprise that her older son, Stephan, had been a student in one of my classes in 1980. He knew nothing of his mother's heroic past.

THE RESISTANCE FIGHTERS OF "DÉFENSE DE LA FRANCE"

Interview with Hélène Viannay[30] (3 juillet 2003)

Hélène Mordkovich Viannay[31] was the daughter of Russian Revolutionaries and a student of natural sciences at the Sorbonne. From the very beginning of the Occupation, the sight of flags with swastikas all over France enraged her, so she took action. "I typed tracts with five carbon copies each and put them in people's mailboxes. It was pointless, but it made me feel better to be doing something." She volunteered to host refugees from northern Europe at the Lilas swimming pool in Paris, which had been transformed into a refugee center.

She met Philippe Viannay, a practicing Catholic who was studying for the *Agrégation* (high level Competitive Examination for Teachers) in philosophy. He sincerely believed that Pétain was playing for both sides and would eventually save France. Hélène strongly disagreed, but when Philippe Viannay told her he was going to publish an underground newspaper and asked for her help, she said yes, "for the pleasure of doing something illicit under the nose of the French and German police." Despite their

---

[30]Mrs. Viannay died on December 25, 2006.

[31]Since my interview with her, two books that contain interviews with Hélène Viannay have been published. *Elles et Eux de la Résistance*, narratives presented by Caroline Langlois and Michel Reynaud. Editions Tirésias, 2003 (pp. 11-22) and *La France résistante* by Alain Vincenot. Editions des Syrtes, 2004 (pp. 128-135). Clarisse Feletin published a biography entitled *Hélène Viannay*, Editions Pascal, 2004. Philippe Viannay wrote *Du bon usage de la France*. Editions Ramsay, 1988. See also 1939-1945 *Combats de femmes*, edited by Evelyne Morin-Rotureau. Editions Autrement. No. 74. 2001 (pp. 134-141).

divergent viewpoints, Hélène and Philippe got married in 1942. Thus, Hélène was rid of her Jewish last name.

While studying, she worked as a laboratory assistant in the Geology department. She worked on publishing the newspaper, *Défense de la France,* with Philippe Viannay and an escaped Jewish prisoner named Robert Salmon. She typed the articles on a typewriter, but there was no money to print them. Who could they ask for funds? Philippe turned to the Catholic officers who were his instructors during his military training, but they refused to help.

He then thought of the wealthy gas tycoon, Lebon, whom he had helped to organize summer camps before the war. Lebon was set on "enlightening the French people," so the idea of an underground newspaper filled him with enthusiasm. Lebon agreed to finance the newspaper and bought a Czech printing press (rotaprint) they baptized Simone. He provided all the supplies they needed: stencils, ink, paper. "It was marvelous that he paid for everything!"

There was, however, the ever-present danger. They had to move constantly with the machine to avoid being caught. The clandestine journalists finally ended up moving to the cellar of a laboratory building in the Sorbonne where Hélène worked. They stayed there for over a year. They did their own printing, since Philippe did not want to take the risk of involving any outside printers. Hélène and the *Défense de la France* team would work three nights per week, sleep for two hours and then go to their regular jobs during the day. The curfew prevented them from being out in the street from 11pm to 5am, "so we were obligated to stay all night. It was very difficult three nights per week, since we were also working all day. We went home at 5am, and we were not eating very well either."

FRENCH HEROINES, 1940-1945
Interview with Hélène Viannay (3 juillet 2003)

For a long time, Hélène helped print the underground newspaper, but later she regretted never having authored any of the articles herself. "The newspaper was pro-Pétain, which was far from my sentiment. If I had given my personal opinion, it would have been interesting to have two diametrically opposing views in the same newspaper." However, unlike the others, who had literary minds, Hélène was a scientist. "I felt they stood head and shoulders above me."

One night while they were printing, they suddenly heard a noise. Philippe looked through the keyhole and at that moment he got a nosebleed. "There was so much blood that it was about to flow under the door. We had to do something to stop the bleeding so that no one would know we were there." They exited through another door. "We ended up in the spacious underground hallways and began exploring them. We kept walking...they were endless!" They found a key and made a spare to be able to come and go as they pleased.

They were reported several times, but never caught. One day they were transporting the rotaprint to the Neuilly apartment of Philippe's parents, who were not home. As they were setting it up in the bathroom, one of Philippe's brothers, who was in the military, warned them that someone had blown the whistle and they should flee. Hélène thought he was just saying that out of fear. "However, two weeks later, the police actually showed up." Luckily, the group had left by then.

They hired students and professors they knew to print and distribute the paper. On July 20, 1943, Elio Marongin, a medical student who delivered the newspaper, sold them out. He was a member of the Bonny Laffont gang who were working for the Germans. "He went directly to the police regularly to reveal what he saw and get paid. He betrayed the entire delivery team, but none of the higher levels because, luckily, they were well compartmentalized. He could not get to the members of the management committee, the printers or typists. Unfortunately, he got a lot of young people arrested at the *'Au Vœu de Louis XIII'* bookstore, our distribution center on rue Bonaparte. Many of those young people were deported and killed. "These were the words of Geneviève de Gaulle, who was among those arrested that day: 'We are young; we are crossing the threshold of destiny. From here on in, life itself turns topsy-turvy.'"

During the July 1943 arrests, Hélène was in the hospital, having just given birth to her son. The director of the maternity ward told her to leave immediately. She understood, asked for an ambulance and took refuge at a friend's house.

Hélène was nursing her baby, but the shock of hearing about the arrests abruptly cut off her milk supply. She needed a milk ration card from the city hall, but her name was on a wanted list. "I had to give sugar water to my baby for two days. Then I found some milk on the black market, and my milk supply came back about two weeks later."

She tried to continue her activities in the Resistance, which was difficult while taking care of her child. "I was no longer doing anything," she told me. "I participated in meetings, and that's it. I corrected texts, typed them out, but I did not go to work with the others." In order to do some work for the movement, she sometimes entrusted her baby to Jacqueline Pardon[32] who remained a good friend of hers.

---

[32]See my interview with her in this book.

FRENCH HEROINES, 1940-1945
Interview with Hélène Viannay (3 juillet 2003)

After the war, she went through tough times. A year and a half after the Liberation, the newspaper became "a mundane paper." It was called *France-Soir* and had a wide circulation. Philippe, the director, was fired. The Viannays were suddenly broke. Philippe then created the *Centre de formation des journalistes* (Journalist Training Center) and the *Centre Nautique des Glénans*[33] where Hélène worked as a volunteer. "I headed the Centre for twenty years." Little by little, their situation improved. They both started earning salaries and had another child.

Hélène separated from her husband[34]. In 1991, she created the *Prix Philippe Viannay, "Défense de la France,"* a history prize awarded each year, in France or in Europe. "It takes place in the *Sénat*; it is a lovely event."

In 2003, Hélène attained a state of harmony with her past. "The Resistance marks you for life. I wonder what image I would have of myself now if I had not been in the Resistance. It is unthinkable."

---

[33]Hélène told me that this center was remarkable, due in large part to the Resistance. At the outset, "we played volleyball and bridge, had swimming contests and theater performances, learned about the sea and the theory of navigation." Then, the center grew: "It became the biggest sailing and cruising school and it still exists today."
[34]He died in 1986.

FRENCH HEROINES, 1940-1945
Interview with Hélène Viannay (3 juillet 2003)

Interview with Jacqueline Pardon[35] *(July 3, 2002)*

Jacqueline Pardon received her education at Notre Dame de Sion[36], an establishment for girls from well-to-do families. She told me, "This may be of interest to you personally: in addition to the school, they also had a program for the conversion of Jews." In her second to last year of school, she met the Jesuit Father de Montcheuil. He had spent six years in Germany. He spoke to the students of Notre Dame de Sion about Hitler and the persecution of Jews. Jacqueline listened attentively. "I learned about Nazism before many French people."

In 1939-40, her father was drafted. The family took refuge in Normandy. Jacqueline enrolled in the college of philosophy in Caen and spent her time with Catholic students. During France's great debacle of June 1940, she and her sister found themselves in the midst of it all, on their bikes. "Gunfire rained down from the planes. It was terrifying." When the armistice was announced, she felt relief (she had been on the road, "in the chaos"). However, her feelings quickly changed.

In November 1940, Jacqueline Pardon began studying for a bachelor's degree in philosophy at the Sorbonne. A year later, in a class taught by Philippe Viannay and Robert Salmon, she gave a presentation on "the love of danger." Impressed by her report, Philippe Viannay told her about the creation of his illicit journal, *Défense de la France*, and asked her if she wanted to participate. She spontaneously agreed, thrilled at the opportunity to give her life meaning.

---

[35]Jacqueline Pardon died on January 20th, 2009.

[36]She added that Sion had been founded by two Jews, the Ratisbonne brothers, who had seen an apparition of the Virgin Mary. She had told them that the curse against the Jews had ended. How wrong she had been!

As one of the movement's founding members, she was involved in all of its aspects. She recruited carriers and she distributed the newspaper herself. It was quite broadly circulated. "I used typographical typesettings to create metal cuts which I then printed on a small offset printing press. I made false papers."

In February 1943, having refused to participate in Germany's forced labor program (*Service du Travail Obligatoire*)[37], Philippe Viannay went underground. Jacqueline hid him and his wife Hélène at the home of her grandparents (who had fled to Normandy) on the *rue d'Alésia* in Paris. "I moved in with them. There was an old distillery through whose roof we could escape. We were able to make our metal cuts for printing. The house became our headquarters. I was able to write for the paper." They distributed the newspaper openly in the metro all day long. They would hurry down a busy metro station, hand out the newspaper to commuters, then hasten through the long corridors into another station and take another metro.

On July 20th, 1943, Jacqueline received a phone call from a messenger of the Viannay family informing her that Philippe's brother, Hubert Viannay, was ill. The message was a code. Hubert was due to cross the Spanish border the next day, but first he had to say farewell to his fellow newspaper carriers at the bookshop on *rue Bonaparte*, "which served as our primary mailbox. So I ran over there to warn him not to go home, as the Germans were waiting for him there."

As bad luck would have it, Jacqueline was caught by Bonny of the Bonny-Laffont gang. "I was not the only one. Hubert

---

[37]The STO, established in 1942, forcibly recruited young French people to go work in German factories. In 1943, facing a shortage of workers, Germany required even more French workers, promising to liberate one POW for three Frenchmen sent to Germany. The promise was not kept.

Viannay, Geneviève de Gaulle and some of the newspaper distributors were captured as well. We had been sold out." Jacqueline was the one who had recruited Geneviève de Gaulle, the General's niece, into her Resistance movement, as they were members of the same Catholic circles. "She had written two major articles on her uncle in the newspaper and signed them 'Gallia.' Her articles swayed Philippe Viannay towards Gaullism."

Jacqueline had very few compromising documents on her. Unfortunately, the person who informed on them had photographed Jacqueline. "First, they took us to the interrogation center on *place des Etats-Unis*, where I was recognized by one of the interrogators. I had seen him on July 14th (Bastille Day) in the metro when we were openly handing out newspapers." Then she was taken to the German Gestapo headquarters on *rue des Saussaies*, where she was locked in a closet and told she would be tortured the next day. This did not scare her, however. On the contrary, she slept like a baby from 7:30pm to 9am. Sometimes even extreme exhaustion has its benefits.

By some stroke of luck, she was not tortured. "The Germans quickly realized that we were not Communists, but simply idealist and patriotic students." However, Jacqueline was not yet out of her predicament: she was taken to the Fresnes prison, where she was put in a cell with three other women who were there for very diverse reasons. "One of them was a prostitute who had been arrested for having slapped Hitler 'right in the kisser' on a German poster. She turned out to be my best cell-mate. She shared her Red Cross provision package with me when I was deprived of mine for disobedience."

Every day for twelve days, Jacqueline went to the prison on the *rue des Saussaies* to be interrogated. On her first trip there, she saw Jacques Lusseyran, the leader of the group "Volontaires de la Liberté,"[38] who also oversaw the distribution of *Défense de la France*. "He was a young, brilliant student of Khâgne, a very prestigious preparatory school, who had lost his eyesight in an accident. He was being escorted by two German soldiers to the prison van." She moved closer to him and they were put in the same vehicle. "We were able to speak, exchange some information and deduce who had betrayed us. Since we knew what the traitor, Elio Marongin, knew, we were able to give the Germans only some information and conceal the rest."

At the Fresnes prison, Jacqueline, who feared nothing, set up news broadcasts. At noon, while the guards changed, she climbed up to her cell's high casement window, opened it and yelled, "This is Jacqueline from *Défense de la France*. Here is the news for the day." She gathered the information from new arrivals, going from cell to cell. By the time she heard the clanking keys of the approaching guard, she was already back on the ground. She was taking a huge risk, as the guards were quickly onto her and caught her one day in the middle of a broadcast. She was immediately put in solitary confinement. "That was not fun. I had just one piece of bread to eat and I slept on the wet cement. On November 11th[39] I heard the prisoners singing the *Marseillaise*."

Ten days later, she was transferred to a cell with barred windows. Through the pipes, she overheard another prisoner being forced to talk in exchange for her baby's life. Jacqueline

---

[38]They were a group of high school students from the major lycées of Paris who helped distribute many copies of the newspaper *Défense de la France*.
[39]WWI Armistice Day. (Translator's Note)

was absolutely horrified. She stayed for three weeks in that cell, where she did not get enough to eat and was not allowed to do anything at all. "But mother nature designs things well. I slept for 18 hours per day until they took me out of that cell and to *rue des Saussaies*, where they told me they were liberating me. It was a few days before Christmas, and the Germans were granting pardons." She was free, but not completely, as she was being followed. The Gestapo were hoping she would unwittingly lead them to the leaders of her movement.

She took endless precautions to lose her trackers, escape from their watchful eyes and join Philippe Viannay, who hid her in his house for a month. More motivated than ever to lead the battle against the occupying force, she became involved in another Resistance activity. "I left with Claude Monod, head of the F.F.I. of the Burgundy and Franche-Comté regions to work as his deputy in the regional Maquis. Claude was in charge of coordinating the Maquis actions in those regions. We settled in the Maquis of Aignay-le-Duc, northwest of Dijon. The county was fully controlled by the Resistance movement. I was the command post liaison. I received all the messages, by phone and in person. Many Postal employees were on our side. By the end, I was constantly lying on the floor next to the phone." She added, "Our efforts led to the liberation of Dijon on September 11, 1944."

They had created the command post jointly with the regional military delegate from London, whom their Maquis cell had parachuted in. Jacqueline again took on a secretarial role rather than taking up arms. She had learned to decode messages with her radio.[40]

---

[40]"Thanks to the radio, on the 5th of June we received the news that the Allies would land in Normandy on June 6th, 1944. We were thus able to warn all of the Maquis cells to set up a plan to sabotage all railroads and roads."

One night around June 10th, two Canadian motorcyclists arrived, having crossed a large part of France that was still occupied, to join the Maquis. They were astonished to find a woman alone guarding the command post.

Their Maquis carried out several important operations: the capture of Châtillon-sur-Seine with the help of General Leclerc's troops; the capture of Dijon with the troops of General Delattre de Tassigny; the junction between the two armies west of Châtillon, and regular attacks of German convoys on the roads. Jacqueline had prepared a parachuting in that area, albeit unsuccessfully. She organized the sabotage of railways to prevent any movement towards Germany. "The railroads were sabotaged so often that we would take our bicycles with us on the trains. We knew exactly when and where the train would blow up, so before that moment, we would get off the train and continue by bike."

Some episodes of life in the Maquis were difficult to bear, such as the execution of men who turned out to be traitors or the death sentence of the Dijon police chief, who had been kidnapped from the city by Maquis members. "We were tough, first and foremost on ourselves. I was prepared to sacrifice my life and did not expect to survive the war."

Once Jacqueline had completed her operations, she came back to Paris. The war was not over, however, and she requested an intelligence mission on the territory of Belfort, which remained occupied. She had to pass illicitly through Switzerland before entering Belfort. There was a large open field to cross. "The seven people who had passed before me had been shot by German patrols. I climbed over the barbed wire and ran into two German soldiers who had their backs turned. I retraced my steps through dry leaves, which crackled. I then took the advice of my Swiss agents and moved forward while the Germans were doing the rounds of a neighboring farm. I have never been so scared in my life!"

Jacqueline's task was to find people who would be willing to have a radio transmitter. She walked from the Belfort border, as any other means of transport would have required a permit and the army could requisition any vehicle. She did not succeed, but it did not make much of a difference, since the territory was freed shortly afterwards. The Allied forces liberated western Germany and the deportation camps. Unfortunately, however, the deportees remained trapped in the camps where typhus was rampant. Philippe Viannay, with the help of Madame Le Faucheux[41], managed to organize repatriation missions. Jacqueline was recruited as a lieutenant and left for the British zone. "That was how I ended up in Neuengamme, near Hamburg, Germany and saw the inside of the Bergen-Belsen camp, with the moribund prisoners still in their cells. They were throwing the dead bodies, men's and women's, into a mass grave. I saw the huge pit under the open sky: a nightmarish vision of horror."

After the war, she continued working for *Défense de la France*, in the publishing house created by Philippe Viannay. For three or four years, she was a board member of *France-Soir*, "until the paper was acquired by Hachette."

---

[41]"She was an extraordinary woman. After the Liberation, her husband became the CEO of Renault, which provided all of the French army's trucks. I attended a meeting with one of the army generals. Marie-Hélène Le Faucheux had told them that if they did not allow the organization of repatriation missions in the main camps, Renault would no longer supply them with trucks."

Jacqueline married Jacques Lusseyran[42] upon his return from the Buchenwald camp. He was the blind man she had met in the prison van when she was arrested. "Jacques became a professor, mainly in schools for foreign students. He held lectures and wrote books. I had to work with him until the very end while also taking care of my three children.

---

[42]I must note that not only is Jacqueline Pardon omitted from the *Dictionnaire historique de la Résistance*, but her name is not even mentioned in the article on Jacques Lusseyran (pp. 469-470).

Interview with Jacqueline Marié Fleury
(July 1st, 2002)

I met Jacqueline Fleury[43] in Paris, in one of the offices of the ADIR.[44] In 1939, she was a 15-year-old high school student living in Versailles with her family. On October 24th, 1940, Pétain and Hitler shook hands in Montoire and announced their "collaboration." This horrified Jacqueline's parents, who had survived the ordeal of World War I. Jacqueline Fleury's grandmother and aunt had been prisoners in Germany and her maternal grandfather had been deported. "He had suffered atrociously and for four years, he had kept a journal which was much talked about in my family. Little had been said about the experience of civilians in the first World War."

As the Germans pillaged France, Jacqueline remembers standing in line at the Versailles market with her mother, and coming back at 8am empty-handed. "When we were able to find a leek and two carrots, we were ecstatic."

In 1940, 16-year-old Jacqueline began her resistance, as did many young people, by distributing small tracts which symbolized their rejection of the occupying force. She showed me a picture her brother, Pierre Marié, had drawn of a soldier smashing the Château of Versailles. She was quickly contacted by one of her teachers to participate in "very sporadic" actions. "That teacher

---

[43]Jacqueline Fleury wrote a testimonial in the newspaper *Le Lien*, which she kindly sent me. It was published in two different books. The first is in a text entitled, *1939-1945: combats de femmes. Françaises et Allemandes, les oubliées de l'histoire*, Editions Autrement – collection Mémoires no. 74, 2001 (pp. 142-156). The second is in *Bulletin des Amitiés de la Résistance*. No. 17, June 2005.

[44]National Association of Former Interned and Deported Women of the Resistance. (Translator's note)

scared me a little. She was strongly Gaullist and wore the Cross of Lorraine[45] on her coat. I later joined a few other Versailles lycée students who were in the *Défense de la France* movement. Our role was to carry and distribute the movement's newspaper in the region. Our group delivered to Renault's factories, as well as Versailles and the surrounding regions."

The mission was dangerous. Jacqueline only knew one person from the group's core. "While commuting, we risked arrest, in Paris and in the metro, especially in stations rife with French and German police. The Gestapo was our greatest danger." For their safety, they had to observe certain rules: "Never travel in groups in the same metro car, despite our innocent appearance (white ankle socks, school bag, backpack), to avoid multiple arrests; never walk around in the city after curfew; always look as neutral as possible so as not to attract attention. I was young and looked like a little girl." Jacqueline took note of doorways along her route where she could hide if need be. "When I heard the boots of patrolling German soldiers, I hid behind one of those doors."

There were arrests at *Défense de la France*, notably of many of its members in Versailles. Jacqueline then left the movement and became a liaison in the intelligence network *Mithridate,* which her brother had joined in 1941. He had managed to steal several maps of the Atlantic wall[46] from the Château de La Maye in Versailles. "I recopied the maps on carbon paper, then they were transmitted to London through the back shop of a small building. I also looked for places to give Mithridate radio transmissions."

---

[45]The heraldic cross of Lorraine, a cross with two horizontal bars, official symbol of the Free French Forces under Charles de Gaulle. (Translator's note)

[46]A wall of coastal fortifications built by the Germans. The maps showed the ports, the North Sea and all the fortifications built along the wall.

French Heroines, 1940-1945
Interview with Jacqueline Marié Fleury (July 1st, 2002)

The documents were passed along by her brother through the director of a Berlitz school and then transported to the UK in small Lysanders[47].

Jacqueline's entire family joined the Resistance. Her parents hid "young people wanted by the Gestapo. They hosted *Mithridate* radio emissions and meetings with members of the network. My father was a member of the Civil and Military Organization (OCM) in the northern zone."

On February 3rd, 1944, the Gestapo banged on the Marié family's door. Jacqueline and her brother were out, but their mother was able to warn them. The son was wanted and went into hiding, moving from place to place with his sister's help. She was later arrested along with her parents. "We were placed in solitary confinement at the Fresnes prison and subjected to interrogations, beatings, bathtub torture[48] and convoys."

On August 15th, 1944: Jacqueline's first transport began. She was taken by bus to the Pantin train station in Paris. A convoy of 57,000 men and women, separated by gender, were heading for Ravensbrück. There was no mixing of the sexes, although this did not make the experience any less inhumane. One hundred women of all ages, many of whom had undergone torture, were crammed into the train car. One had been dismembered; another had had her nails ripped out. "They gave us a big drum of water, and another drum to use as a bathroom and the doors closed. It was very hot. The train shook us and we fell all over each other. Luckily, everyone was cooperative. The younger women helped the eldest."

---

[47]Lysanders were small, usually one-man, British aircraft.

[48]"They put you in dirty water that had already been used to torture others. They dunked you in, until you lost consciousness, then they lifted you out and tried to make you talk, and repeated the same process over and over again."

All was dark and quiet when the train stopped[49]. Jacqueline was filled with apprehension. No one knew what to expect. Suddenly, a voice pierced the disquieting silence. "One of the women was singing Schubert's Ave Maria. Her voice was magnificent. We listened to that song as if it was our last."

The 600 French women were told to exit the cars and line up in columns of five people each. They walked, escorted by armed SS soldiers, for over four miles, some carrying their luggage. They had nothing to drink as they walked in the torrid heat. "People watched us go by with horror. Some held out water for us, but they were kicked out of the way." The crossed the Marne River and were once again squeezed into the cattle cars and locked up until they reached the German border. "We did not know where we were going. We discussed the most ludicrous conjectures. The train stopped for a long time." The men's cars were detached. "We were in Weimar near the Buchenwald camp, where the male prisoners were going." Something very moving happened at that moment. "On the platform, the men sang a Farewell song to us, and we replied from inside the train cars. I will take that memory with me to my grave. Our convoy lasted for seven days and seven night."

Ravensbrück: they discovered the "aufsherinnen," the female SS officers with German Shepherds trained to bite. They crossed the city of Fürstenberg, "where small curtains swayed behind a window here and there." The deportees arrived at a large gate and entered a vast open area which was the Ravensbrück camp. They saw women with shaved heads in striped dresses. "We thought, 'this is not possible.' One of the women who spoke German asked

---

[49]The women later found out that at that moment, they were stuck inside a tunnel at the beginning of a bridge crossing the Marne River, as the Maquis had bombed the bridge.

that we be given some water. We saw two shaved women wearing some sort of wooden platform shoes and dragging a large hose. We thought we would be able to drink, but they just sprayed the entire roll call area and we did not receive a drop."

The Frenchwomen who were already at the camp came up to them and asked them for food, saying, "Rest assured they will take everything from you and tomorrow you will look exactly like us." Jacqueline and her fellow travelers were stripped of everything and taken to the showers. They were given "rags" which transformed them "into scarecrows marked with red triangles (for political prisoners) with an 'F' meaning French." Jacqueline received a pair of shoes that were much too big for her. She found her mother with her clothing in tatters. She was devastated to find out that her mother had also been subjected to interrogations and the bathtub torture.

"A somber, Dantean atmosphere reigned in Ravensbrück." The women were squashed into a barrack where they slept three or four to a bed, "like sardines." "We stepped on hands, on heads; we heard screams." They had medical inspections. "They made us strip naked to look at our teeth, in front of the laughing SS officers." They had to rise at 3:30am, received a black liquid that was supposed to be coffee and subjected to endless roll calls." They were quarantined, but very soon they were sent to work in the Kommandos[50].

Entire trainloads of "everything you can possibly imagine arrived and we had to unload them." The work was exhausting. Babies were dying. Young girls were used for medical experiments. Everyone had lice and bedbugs. At one point, Jacqueline suffered from dysentery. She was taken to the "Revier"

---

[50]The labor annexes of the concentration camps. (Translator's note)

(infirmary), which remains for her "an indescribably memory." She shared a 28-inch (smaller than twin-size) bed with one woman who was spitting blood and another who was dying.

Jacqueline, her mother and other Frenchwomen were "housed" in Block #24, but while she was at the "Revier," part of the group was moved elsewhere. Her mother managed to get Jacqueline out of the infirmary by giving her bread to a Frenchwoman who worked in the camp office. After several roll calls where I was "shoved away with swinging clubs and dogs towards the old women who were to stay there, I was finally called with the last of the last. My heart racing, I stumbled to join the column of women exiting through the gate."

Her second transport was to the small camp of Torgau, which housed a shell recycling factory. "We had said we did not want to work for the Great Reich. We thought we would be treated like prisoners of war, but nothing changed." Jacqueline's task was to put the shells into acid, wearing no protective clothing. Her mother peeled vegetables in the kitchen.

Her third transport was towards Abteroda, near the city of Eisenach, "J.S. Bach's birthplace." The factory in the Black Forest manufactured V2 missiles. "When flying fortresses bombarded overhead, we were locked above the factory where we lived, and we slept on the floor." Jacqueline and her fellow laborers once again refused to work for the Nazis. They tried sabotage: "We had to verify a part about the size of a hand, with lots of screwed-on thingamajigs. We had to make sure everything was working. We had two boxes, one for working pieces and the other for defective ones. We were watched every second. Sometimes we would put a working part in the box of defective ones and a defective one in the box for working ones." The other women blew up their machine, which blocked progress.

On New Year's Eve, while the Germans were having "a shindig," Jacqueline and the other women made a Nativity scene with bits of dresses, straw and paper they illicitly brought from the factory. "That Nativity scene was not the most beautiful one I had ever seen, but it was the most extraordinary one." One can only imagine how distressed these women were, especially those who had been forced to abandon their children. "I think there was not a single one who did not cry that night."

On January 1st, it was snowing and unbearably cold. They were all getting more and more emaciated. Jacqueline was pained to see her mother in a pitiful state. The poor woman was at the end of her rope, and then an unexpected gesture of kindness came from a German guard: the *aufsehrin* allowed another prisoner, upon her request, to replace Jacqueline's mother. "That was really wonderful. I saw that friend a lot after we returned home."

Abteroda was controlled by the commander of Buchenwald, who came one day to inspect their work. He had "heard that the Frenchwomen were very bad workers." They were sent to another work camp.

Her fourth transport was once again in cattle cars. The cold was worse than ever. They arrived at the Markkleeberg camp, near Leipzig, where there was a small factory that made rockets. 250 Frenchwomen were sent to do very arduous work. "We had to extract gravel with our feet in the water. This was in early 1945; we were undernourished and exhausted. We had nothing to wash with and no change of clothing. We had to cut down trees in the forest or, most unbearably, unload wagons of coal all day long. In the camp, there were various chores, the worst of which was emptying the latrines with shovels. In the evening, we collapsed onto our mattresses without undressing and had to start all over again in the morning. Dragging the huge containers of soup or 'coffee' was torture, as we had to run with them."

Jacqueline witnessed the bombing of Germany, which overjoyed her. On April 13th, "the march of death" began. She left the Markkleeberg camp. They had to line up in columns five by five. The women were allowed to put their sick companions on huge wagons with the packages of the SS. They walked until May 9th, eating grass and drinking from puddles. Their feet were bloodied. The strongest helped the weakest. Jacqueline and her mother shared everything with two friends they had met at Ravensbruck. "If we found a blade of grass, we cut it into four pieces." They remained together and finally escaped. They hid in some mine workers' tool shed. They were found by French POWs. "They saved our lives. They gave us a bit of milk and clothes."

On May 9th, Red Army soldiers entered Germany from the southeast. Some of Jacqueline's companions were raped by them. Jacqueline and her small group were taken to Koenigstein. "It was a fortress that housed all the POWs and superior officers who took us under their wing and asked the American Red Cross to allow us to be the first to be transferred to the American zone for medical treatment."

Then they arrived at the Lutetia hotel, of which Jacqueline has negative memories. Many people asked them, "'Did you know so-and-so?' Some of the women there were all dolled up. To them, we were weird. We felt like aliens."

FRENCH HEROINES, 1940-1945
Interview with Jacqueline Marié Fleury (July 1st, 2002)

In early June, 1945, back in Versailles, Jacqueline's first thought was of her father,[51] who must have had an awful experience. He was a diabetic and could not live without insulin. The house was still standing. "My father opened the door. We had an amazing, tear-filled reunion." However, the government of Versailles did not deem this family of Resistance fighters worthy of notice. Jacqueline has never forgiven them.

For a while, she continued to study both law and social work, and then got married in 1946. "My biggest joy was the birth of my first child. The executioners had not triumphed; life was starting again."

---

[51]"He had been in the convoy we had left behind in Weimar. He was at Buchenwald." Her brother continued to fight in the Resistance and luckily avoided arrest.

FRENCH HEROINES, 1940-1945
Interview with Jacqueline Marié Fleury (July 1st, 2002)

THE RESISTANCE FIGHTERS OF LONDON'S BCRA[52]
Interview with Brigitte Friang (July 22, 2001)

Brigitte Friang's[53] old house is nestled at the end of a cedar-lined lane in the small village of Saignon, 30 miles from Avignon. It was very hot the day we spoke for two hours in her garden, accompanied by the cicadas' song. I had discovered Brigitte thanks to her book, *Regarde-toi qui meurs*.[54]

At the beginning of the German occupation, Brigitte Friang was a sixteen-year-old Catholic schoolgirl. She started tearing down propaganda posters and singing, "Radio Paris lies; Radio Paris has been Germanized." In 1941, shortly before final exams, she was expelled from high school for having engraved, using acid, the V for victory and the Lorraine cross[55] on the windows of her chemistry classroom.

At age 19, Brigitte met 26-year-old Jean-François Clouët des Pesruches. He had arrived by parachute in August and was looking for a secretary to code and decode radio messages and accompany him on important meetings. He preferred having a female associate because two men would be too noticeable. That

---

[52]*Bureau central de Renseignement et d'Action* (Central Office of Information and Action) of de Gaulle's Free France, created in August 1942 and headed by Colonel Passy in London.

[53]Guylaine Guidez wrote several pages about her in *Femmes dans la Guerre 1939-1945* (Perrin, 1989).

[54]This book was first published by Editions Laffont in 1970, followed by several new editions including one by Editions du Félin, sponsored by the association "Résistance, Liberté, Mémoire" in 1997. She was awarded several prizes: "Vérité" in 1970, "Maisons de la Presse" in 1971 and "Maryse Bastié" in 1974.

[55]See translator's note p.86 (interview with J.M. Fleury).

was how Brigitte joined the Air Operations Bureau (BOA), a "network for clandestine paradrops and landings of weapons and agents of London's BCRA." *(Regarde-toi qui meurs,* p. 21).

In Brigitte's own words: "I knew all of the landing grounds and their coordinates, the hiding places and names of our main agents. I also knew all the meeting places and schedules two weeks ahead of time. The phone lines were bugged, so we had to agree in person on our meeting day, time and place ahead of time. We had no other way to contact each other."

She left her family home at a young age because her responsibilities in the Resistance movement would have endangered her parents. "A 19-year-old girl coming home late at night would have attracted attention."

The first task she participated in was deciding the plight of a female member of the network who was seen in the company of a British agent. "Having contacts with another organization was always dangerous." The Germans had been able to catch so many people that way! The woman was questioned. Should they take the precaution of killing her? "I suggested that we give her a chance and we cut off all ties with her. The funny thing is that I saw her after the war. She does not know it, but I may have saved her life."

Moonlight was needed to parachute in weapons and money. Unfortunately, there was a risk that the Gestapo would be alerted by the roar of airplane motors that preceded the airdrops. They discovered many of the landing fields. The main difficulty was "gathering the necessary teams to receive the agents and the containers of weapons, ammunition and money. Men were also needed to surround the landing ground and light it with flashlights or torches to indicate the wind direction. The landing grounds were often poorly asphalted and close to forests or electrical wires.

French Heroines, 1940-1945
Interview with Brigitte Friang (July 22, 2001)

The British pilots had remarkable courage and dexterity."

One night, in Normandy, with her boss, Jean-François Clouët, she was preparing to cross a bridge over a railroad. They were carrying a suitcase with radio controls for the airdrop they were expecting, and they saw a German guard walking towards them. Brigitte whispered to Jean-François, "Put down the suitcase and wrap your arms around me." The guard walked by with a smirk. Brigitte suggested to her boss that he turn back towards the city, then picked up the suitcase herself and crossed the bridge, "under the gaze of the guard who focused mainly on my legs. A woman, especially at that time, elicited less suspicion than a man."

Brigitte always kept her wits about her. One night, she was traveling with her boss to inspect a landing ground near Nantes and bring a suitcase full of documents. The train had sleeping cars, and Clouët asked the conductor if he had one or two berths left. There was a single remaining berth in a compartment for two occupied by a German officer who generously offered to share his compartment with Brigitte. "So I spent the night with a German officer, who behaved like a gentleman. I was laughing to myself, as my suitcase would have interested him greatly. My boss gave me a meaningful wink as he left the compartment."

She also had to deliver an explosive suitcase to the Glacière metro station in the 13th *arrondissement* of Paris. The suitcase had been airdropped from London and contained aircraft radio controls. It was equipped with a security lock: if opened without the right combination, it would detonate. In the metro car, a German officer stared at Brigitte with great interest. "Usually, if a German observed me, I looked straight through him. But this time, I gave him a slight smile. He took it as an invitation. When I got off the metro, he followed me and offered to carry my suitcase. I accepted and we left the metro side by side. Before we parted ways, I thanked the officer. He saluted me with a click of his heels, convinced that although he had not reached the goal he would have aspired from a willing, pretty woman, that he had at least changed one Frenchwoman's opinion of Germans."

Each time Brigitte went to the same region, she changed her style of dress. Thus, the Gestapo did not realize that all of these young ladies were really one and the same. Yet, despite these precautions, she was arrested. During her interrogations, she was constantly obligated to invent solid, infallible alibis that would never have come to her in peacetime. "In these circumstances of extreme stress, there is a sort of mental acceleration, as if you were getting a shot of stimulants. Your brain functions at full speed with bewildering logic."

Brigitte knew how to defend herself. Her father had taught her to fight. "I was very strong." Moreover, her boss had trained her in British self-defense techniques. The main elements of hand-to-hand combat involved knowing how to stab or cut the throat of a guard, and, with tied or free hands, push away a revolver held too close to one's chest or back. "The locks and choke holds, kicks or knee blows, as well as knife use were all very familiar to me." Thanks to her combat instructors, she had full mastery of the violent tactics that men used in fighting.

I could not help but ask Brigitte, "Did you ever use those survival combat skills?" Yes, she said, during her arrest in the Trocadéro garden. She was on her way to a meeting place when she was suddenly surrounded by Gestapo policemen. "I jammed my elbow into the solar plexus of the man in front of me as he cried, 'Hands up, Brigitte!' It was a move I had been taught and it had an immediate effect. The guy fell over backwards. I jumped on him, thinking, 'I'll show them how a Frenchwoman dies.' Silly, wasn't it? What I wanted, really, was to get killed because I was afraid I would crack under torture. As I told you, I knew everything about the Western sector, the coordinates for airdrops and landing grounds, the code phrases announcing operations on the London radio, hiding places for weapons, agents' future meeting places and even the true identity of my boss, his addresses and those of his family members."

The head of the liaison agents of the Eastern Unit of BOA, who had been arrested the day before, had turned her in. He later confessed, "I gave your name because I was sure you would not talk."

"Oh, how kind of you. Thanks a lot!"

She was shot in the hip and the bullet went through her stomach. She was transported to the *Charles Quentin* wing of the *Pitié* hospital, which was originally an insane asylum but during the war it was reserved for "terrorists." Luckily, the SS in charge of that wing, an Austrian, "probably sorely lacking a feminine presence" and moved by this young wounded girl, allowed her to have books that were forbidden and that she hid when the Gestapo came to interrogate her. The Austrian "clanged his boots on the hallway tiles and fiddled with the lock so as to give me time to hide the books under my sheets. He was the one who taught me how to walk again." Admittedly, some SS officers could understand human feelings... and even fall in love.

Brigitte faced the Germans without lowering her gaze, which, she told me, exasperated the authorities. One day, she kicked an SS dog that was harassing her, infuriating the guard. He rushed at her "with a raised fist." She wrote in her book, "I watched him, motionless and clearly indifferent. He turned away."[56] She

---

[56]*Regarde-toi qui meurs*, p. 100.

refused to yield to the SS and got her revenge by laughing up her sleeve at them. "It is delightful to make fun of those who hold your plight in their hands."[57] The Germans were offended by the insolence in her gaze. Not a muscle in her face twitched as she stared at them, but her contempt showed through.

One day, in Czechoslovakia, she managed to drive an SS *aufsherin* crazy just by looking at her with that frozen expression. Brigitte was punished with a week of Kommando labor camp, but, she says, "That's OK; it was fun."[58]

Her derision and tenacity preserved her sanity and dignity. At the hospital where she was taken, when asked by the Gestapo officer where she lived, she replied, "'Under a bridge.' I could not resist that jibe. A doctor was examining me to see if the bullet had pierced my intestines. The doctors and the police exchanged a few words that clearly did not bode well. The doctors left the room and the Gestapo began to beat me with their fists all over, including my stomach and my wound. Luckily there was a clock hanging on the wall and I was thinking, 'Beat away, guys; I know where my boss is at this very moment, but you'll never know!'" She hypnotized herself by staring at that clock, which helped mitigate the pain from the blows. Then, after a futile escape attempt initiated by her network, she was sent to the Fresnes prison and deported to Germany and then to Czechoslovakia.

In Fresnes, Brigitte was never idle. In one of the grooves of the hardwood floor, she found a pencil lead and used it to write in a small prayer book she had received from the prison chaplain. She wrote between its lines to help her remember, so as not to deform her story "afterwards." At the camp, she jotted down notes

---

[57]Idem, p. 100.
[58]*Regarde-toi qui meurs,* p. 114.

on scraps of paper which she slipped inside the hems of her dress and jacket. That way she was able to record many events and dates with precision. She knew that her "memory would do its job" and she wanted "to relate the exact truth to the maximum extent possible. You know, memory is always selective." She thus ended up writing the bulk of her book immediately upon her return from Germany.

From Fresnes, she and her fellow prisoners were taken to the Romainville fort, then to Ravensbrück in Germany, where they were quarantined for 2 weeks. In Romainville, Brigitte met Lou Peters, a Frenchwoman with whom she formed "a fast friendship." "Lou Peters had an unattractive face, illuminated by beautiful blue eyes." The other women surrounded the new arrivals, hungry for information. It was hot. "I suddenly felt unwell. Lou dragged me to the dormitory, put me on a bed and brought me water." Later, at Ravensbrück, Brigitte was to receive fifty blows with a wooden stick as punishment for an act of provocation[59], which could have been fatal in her extremely weakened state. Lou went to see the head of their unit, a Polish woman, and asked her to exchange numbers with Brigitte to be beaten in her place. It was a magnificent gesture done for a woman she barely knew.

After Ravensbrück, she was sent to the Zwodau camp in Czechoslovakia. There, despite the searing pain of her stomach wound, Brigitte was forced to throw shovelfuls of stones into a wagon. She also had to level and pave roads. "But the worst part was carrying rails. Railway tracks are very heavy, even for ten or

---

[59]In her book, Brigitte Friang tells about how, in the Ravensbrück camp, she was caught by the guards playing bridge with forbidden cards. Her fellow players hid their cards, but Brigitte kept hers in the open, pretending to continue to play. She thus earned "a punishment few survived." (*Regarde-toi qui meurs*, p. 119).

101

twenty women!" She was then assigned to the task of controlling the quality of parts in a factory. She continued her rebellion through sabotage: "I had to check cogwheels. I put the working ones in the box of unusable ones. When they told me to mark all the parts, I engraved the Lorraine cross on them. Then I created a bottleneck in the assembly line and was dismissed." Her lungs gave out and she spent several months in the infirmary. Finally, on April 16, 1945, she was condemned to join a column of people heading for the Dachau gas chambers.

Meanwhile, the beleaguered German forces were being squeezed by the Soviet troops from the east and by General Patton's tanks from the west. The women faced a grueling march of 300 miles—about 14 miles per day. Of the 1500 women who had left Zwodau on April 16, 1945, only 200 survivors remained the day Brigitte and two other deportees managed to escape. Ironically, that day was May 8, 1945—Victory day! But cannon fire still reverberated in Bohemia.

On May 21, 1945, Brigitte returned to her family home. She was physically debilitated and mentally dejected. She thought of suicide, or of entering a convent. "The world seemed insignificant, like flies buzzing around in a bell jar. What saved me was my curiosity about life and the future."

She dedicated her book to André Malraux, because she was "greatly impressed by his intelligence and encyclopedic knowledge," she said. "I worked with him for several years, first as a public relations agent in a movement supporting General de Gaulle, then when Malraux was a deputy minister under the General, who was president of the Provisional government of the French Republic at the time." After the Liberation, Brigitte went to Indochina as a wartime correspondent.

Interview with Jeanne Bohec (June 26, 2001)

Jeanne Bohec lives in the 18th *arrondissement* of Paris, in a ground floor apartment surrounded by greenery and flowers. The museum-like interior is filled with antique furniture and countless photos of General de Gaulle. She is the author of a book, *La Plastiqueuse à bicyclette*[60] which she dedicated to the "Great Charles".

Jeanne was born in Brittany in 1919, a true *Breton* by birth and lineage. Her role model was her father, who was a military agent in charge of wartime equipment and worked for eight years on submarines.

Her dream was to fight against France's enemies, but she did not think she would ever have that opportunity. "Even though everyone was predicting war, it was not a woman's place, unless she was a nurse." (*La plastiqueuse à bicyclette* p. 12). Just to be prepared, however, she took public courses in self-defense and first aid. She also studied chemistry for a year and a half. When one of her teachers announced that a factory in Brest was seeking a Chemist's assistant, she jumped at the chance. The job involved making explosives for shells.

In 1940, the armistice made her seethe with rage. "It was inadmissible. They should have continued to fight!" Having worked in the gunpowder factory in Brest, she was afraid of being forced to work for the Germans. She spoke some English, so on June 18th, although she did not hear General de Gaulle's call to arms, she took a boat from Brest to England to continue to fight

---

[60]This book was first published in 1975 by Mercure de France; a second edition was published by Editions du Félin in 1999, sponsored by the association "Résistance, Liberté, Mémoire." She was awarded the *Millepierres* prize in 2000.

against Germany. Upon her arrival in London, she was placed in a family as a female companion, a position she strongly disliked. On July 14th (Bastille Day) she participated in a huge demonstration in Trafalgar Square with General de Gaulle. She thus met with members of the Free French Forces, who would not accept a female member. British women, however, were mobilized in the army, navy and air force[61].

In December 1940, the French "*Corps féminin des Volontaires françaises*"[62] was created, modeled on the ATS. Jeanne enlisted on January 6, 1941 and remained in the *Corps* until 1943. She explained that the name was often mocked, as "corps féminin" also means "female body." The organization was later renamed "*Corps des Volontaires Françaises*"[63]. In Bournemouth, she had two weeks of British-style training. There was a great deal of marching, which was hard on her "short legs." She learned various maneuvers for unarmed soldiers.

I asked Jeanne if the British had a different attitude towards women than the French. "It was about the same. Perhaps they were a bit ahead of us, since they accepted women in the ATS, but, you see, the key word is 'auxiliary.'" They remained in the background, assistants with traditionally "female" roles: cooks, secretaries or nurses. Jeanne quickly received the rank of Corporal. She had to supervise the volunteers' marching, make sure they returned to the barracks and wake them up in the morning.

---

[61]"They had a choice between the A.T.S. (Auxiliary Territorial Service), the Army, WAAF (Women's Auxiliary Air Force), WRNS (Women's Royal Naval Service), and the Land Girls (Women's Land Army, a civilian organization working in the fields)." (*La plastiqueuse à bicyclette*, p. 28).

[62]Female French Volunteer Corps.

[63]French Volunteer Corps.

Jeanne then worked as a secretary in the weaponry unit of the Technical department until the spring of 1942. She was in charge of mail, answering the phone and typing. A research laboratory was established and the work was dangerous: "We had to find easy ways to make explosives or incendiary devices with store-bought products. We also made detonators, or less powerful explosives which explode and burn upon impact."

The BCRA parachuted boys into France to commit sabotage. Jeanne taught them "our little secrets." Later, she came up with the "bright idea" of doing the same thing in France. She turned to the BCRA, whose response was, "No way! No women." Nevertheless, stubborn Jeanne has always obtained what she wanted, even if it took a long time. "I was persistent. I was the first woman accepted by the BCRA to be sent to France. I was the only sabotage instructor in the French Forces of the Interior (FFI)." First, she had to undergo training: pass endurance tests, go through obstacle courses, show team spirit, learn morse code, and use a morse key. She also had to take courses in sabotage to learn to use all sorts of weapons: guns, knives and swords.

She went to parachuting school to learn to jump from the plane, position herself during the fall and land properly. She learned to code, decode and write messages with invisible ink[64]. Her emblem was *"Râteau"* (Rake). She became a sabotage instructor in Brittany with the BOA (Air Operations Bureau), in charge of paradrops and landings. She was parachuted in with money and explosives for the Western region BOA. Upon arrival, she was to say the code phrase, "The boa will coil up and bring you a little one." The receiving committee was stupefied to see a

---

[64]Transparent ink that becomes readable when a reactive substance is applied to the paper.

woman under the parachute. "I was one of the first women paratroopers in France."

Later, Jeanne was sent to form sabotage teams in the Morbihan region. This time, "none of the boys was surprised to see a female instructor. They treated me like one of their own." She also participated in "Le Plan Vert" (the "Green Plan") in that region, which took place from May 7th to 13th, 1944. "The Allies had dreamt up the idea of blowing up all of the railways at the same time, but they wanted to make sure it would work. So they did a test in the Morbihan region. A few weeks before D-Day, on a given day, my students blew up all the railroads. Then I blew one up as well, but there were not enough detonators, so I made some using chemicals. I cut off the railroad that crossed Brittany and my students did the same thing all over the Morbihan region. By the time of the Normandy landings, the British gave the green light for all of France to do the same thing. This Green Plan was very useful, as, at that moment, the Germans who were in southern Brittany headed towards Normandy, but those traveling by train arrived later than those who left on foot."

In early June 1944, Jeanne was asked to participate in a meeting of the Saint Marcel Maquis in the city of Quimper, where she had to prepare paradrops with members of the BOA and pick up the agents and materials. One day, Jeanne told me, she had the fright of her life during a mission she was in charge of in the Morbihan region. She and her partner bicycled out of Quimper, having agreed that if they were arrested, they would pretend not to know each other. "Suddenly, we saw soldiers on horseback coming towards us from both sides of the road. I later found out that they were with Vlasov's Army—Russians working for the Germans. They stopped us and searched us. In my bra, I had code phrases from the BBC to transmit to people in the region. My code sentence to announce the landings was something like: 'The die is cast.' In my bag, they found a Michelin map and asked me, 'Why map?' I replied that I was on my way to see my sick grandmother and that I did not know the way. So they scrutinized the map. I was worried because although the location of the Saint Marcel Maquis was not marked, we had put our fingers on that spot. I thought, 'That's it, they're going to see it,' but they let me go. I got back on my bike and joined my partner, who was waiting for me 600 feet down the road."

In the Maquis, Jeanne wanted to fight using weapons, as she was trained. She told me she had better mastery of them than many of the FFI members. But as long as there were men, women were not allowed to touch weapons. The Germans razed the Maquis and the surrounding area. Jeanne told me proudly that in July 1944, she had the honor of organizing three airdrops in Brittany, which was liberated on August 8th. Jeanne had completed her mission.

She added, "Many women did a great deal that remains unknown. Resistance comprises many actions, both large and small. My poor mother, for example, pierced the tires of a German bicycle in Rennes. That's resistance, even if it did not amount to much."[65]

In February 1945, Jeanne married a Resistance fighter, gave birth to a son and divorced three years later. "When it came to the Resistance and the war, we got along well, but after the war,

---

[65]In 2003, when I interviewed Yvette Farnoux, she also wondered about the definition of Resistance. "I always say that when the concierge of my building took the mail that was addressed to me, she was resisting. She knew what she was doing by taking a letter; she had as much to lose as someone who was wholly engaged."

we no longer saw eye to eye." Did she have any difficulties readapting to civilian life? "Not particularly. I only had trouble getting back into teaching, as I had not finished my studies, so I got in through the back door and ended up becoming a math teacher, which had been my calling since I was a little girl." She was also the Deputy Mayor of the 18th *arrondissement*. "I officiated marriages."

THE COMMUNIST RESISTANCE FIGHTERS
Interview with Raymonde Tillon (June 27, 2002)

Raymonde[66] was born in 1915 and lost her parents at a very young age. She and her nine-year-old sister were placed by their uncle in a religious orphanage in Arcueil, near Paris. The nuns in their dark habits frightened her. "Mother had been so pretty and gentle. I was only five, but I still remember the doorway I came through. The nuns had brown skirts, black veils with narrow bands on their foreheads, and a no-nonsense look. I was in awe. It's a good thing my sister was with me."

At age 13, she learned to sew men's silk shirts. She received a few *centimes*, with the promise of receiving the rest of her money when she came of age. But when her older sister came to pick up her modest nest egg a bit early, the nuns refused to give it to her. Her sister then decided to help 17-year-old Raymonde escape. Raymonde wrote in her book: "Arcueil instilled in me a distaste for locked doors and a passion for freedom and justice." (*J'écris ton nom Liberté*, p. 23).

Having escaped, she took refuge with her older brother, a railway worker, in St. Martin-de-Crau in the south of France. She had left behind "a prison rather than a boarding school." Her brother was a trade union activist. Raymonde often went to his demonstrations, where one day she met the Communist orator Paul Vaillant-Couturier. "I was so enthralled with him that I immediately joined the Communist party. I fell under their spell."

---

[66]Before our interview, Raymonde had published a book, *J'écris ton nom Liberté*. Foreword by Germaine Tillion. Afterword by Charles-Louis Foulon. Paris: Editions du Félin, 2002.

109

FRENCH HEROINES, 1940-1945
Interview with Raymonde Tillon (June 27, 2002)

She started reading the Communist press[67] and felt a growing desire to fight against fascism and social injustice.

At age 20, she married Mr. Nédelec, a Communist widower and leader of the trade union movement. They moved to Marseille and she enrolled in the *Pigier* school to learn shorthand and typing. She and her classmates also helped poor teenagers, taking them hiking in the mountains to keep them busy. She thus helped create the *Union des Jeunes Filles de France[68]*, in Marseille and nation-wide. "There was always the political idea of involving them in the Communist Party, and at the same time, it took them away from their daily grind."

A natural athlete, Raymonde enjoyed basketball, running and swimming. She learned to pilot a plane thanks to the creation of *l'Aviation Populaire[69]*. "That helped me a lot in my ordeals later on." She became involved in the fight against Spanish fascism and helped young refugees from Spain.

She became friends with the mother of her husband's first wife, Agnès Dumay, the daughter of a Communist activist. "She was a mother to me. I adored her and she adored me." Agnès died in November 1938 in a Nazi air strike in Spain. At that moment, Raymonde swore to fight with all her might "against the Hitlerites and their accomplices."

---

[67]Newspaper of the Communist Youth and *L'Avant-Garde*.

[68]The Union of Young Women of France, part of the Communist Youth Movement, was founded by Danielle Casanova in 1936. Raymonde participated in its creation, as she writes in her book, along with "Paulette Laugery and Josette Reybaut" (*J'écris ton nom, Liberté*, p. 29).

[69]Popular Aviation was a free activity created for young people by the Minister of Aviation, Pierre Cot.

Her husband was mobilized and sent to Abidjan in 1939. Prime Minister Edouard Daladier dissolved the Communist party. Twice a month, Raymonde sent packages to political prisoners. She found a job in a furniture factory that had been requisitioned by the army to make crates of shells. She had a child-sized printing press and she and her peers were able to print small pamphlets. On weekends, she raised funds to buy cigarettes for soldiers, which she and her friends then put in the crates of shells along with their pamphlets.

In 1940, she was fired from the furniture factory and found a job in a dry-cleaner's shop. She put up flyers denouncing the occupation and demanding more provisions. "You know," Raymonde told me, "those who did not live through that period cannot imagine true poverty! Everything was looted by the Germans and their collaborators. They were the only ones with full bellies." Her true work was recruiting young women into the Resistance Movement. She kept her network of contacts from 1935-36, when she was working with 15- and 16-year-olds. "The work was no longer the same as in 1936, when I was taking them hiking. These were no Sunday outings."

March 1941: In Marseille, a certain Mancarelli, claiming to have escaped a round-up in Toulon, wormed his way into the group and gained their trust. They all met in Raymonde's apartment, along with two Resistance fighters she was hiding for one night: Maguy Badet from Lyon and Jean Mérot from Paris. The next day at 6am, the police came to arrest them all. Jean climbed out the window and hid on the floor above. The others were imprisoned and then tried in the Toulon naval tribunal in

October 1941. "I was certain the sentence had been determined from the outset," Raymonde declared. Jean was condemned to death; Raymonde and Maguy got 20 years of forced labor.

Thus began Raymonde's prison stays. The first one was at Saint Joseph in Lyon. "The filth in there was awful. There were bedbugs and cockroaches crawling on our faces. Plus, we were mixed in with the common law prisoners." Raymonde revolted against the food and managed to receive canned peas.

The second prison was La Centrale in Rennes. Raymonde worked in a factory that made cellophane bags for stockings. She deliberately did a shoddy pasting job and threw away paper and products the minute the supervisors turned away. She and her peers helped and supported each other, uniting against injustices. Once, the mother of a young man who had been shot, received a dress in a package from her family. The guards cut the dress "so short that it just covered her breasts. They were always afraid we would escape." The victim rebelled against that deplorable act and was to be put in the dungeon. All of her fellow prisoners joined forces to keep her from being punished. They threw stools and their shoes into a corner of the workshop. They pushed the tables together and formed a human chain.

The *Gardes Mobiles de Réserve*, (GMR)[70], a bunch of savage brutes, arrived with the director and ordered them to surrender. The women prisoners sang the *Marseillaise*, the partisans' song and the hymn of the FTP[71]. Fighting broke out between the prisoners and the GMR. The judge proclaimed, "You know that

---

[70]Elite sub-section of the Vichy *Police Nationale*, which had the specific task of actively combating known terrorist organizations. (Translator's note)
[71]*Francs Tireurs et Partisans*, the armed Resistance movement of the French Communist Party. (Translator's note)

we do not tolerate rebellion. Your fellow prisoners rebelled and they were tried and sentenced to death. We have decided you deserve the same treatment." They wanted to argue, and were beaten in retaliation. They were deprived of packages and mail. The woman whose son had been shot was put in solitary confinement with no food. Determined not to back down, the women who worked in the kitchen managed to sneak bowls of hot soup to her every day.

After that month-long episode, Raymonde spent some time in Romainville, and then in Sarrebruck. She refused to work for a while, but, starving, she began sewing in a factory again. She unstitched the military uniforms, worked as slowly as possible and deluded her guards by telling them, "France is the country of *haute couture*, so we are used to doing excellent work. It is well done and there is nothing to find fault with." She then proceeded to sew the snaps and buttons on the wrong sides of the garment.

Raymonde was transferred to Ravensbrück and locked up all day long with the other women. At the beginning, they had no identification numbers, so they were not allowed to go out. "We were cramped like sardines in those cells. There were wooden barracks as far as the eye could see, in a cold and desolate landscape." Raymonde was soon sent to Leipzig, which was administered by the Buchenwald camp. There, she met German workers, deportees and POWs who told her what was going on in the outside world.

She had to galvanize shell cases, which meant being in contact with large basins of acid. The Frenchwomen sabotaged the work. They wreaked havoc in the production process and told the youngest women, "Don't overexert yourselves; go directly to the electric dryer." The shells were not rinsed. Raymonde spun the wheel too fast. "The guards never figured out that the deportees were sabotaging the work. They thought the acid was defective."

Raymonde had received a dress made of thin, transparent fabric. She complained and demanded protective suits for herself and her fellow inmates. "We are not refusing to work, but in France, when factory workers have to handle dangerous chemicals, they receive overalls and they have a right to drink milk every day." The Major replied, "You can have overalls since you are working. As for milk, Madame, we do not even have any for our children." Raymonde retorted, "We are not the ones who declared war. You invaded our territory. If your children have no milk, it's your own fault." The women received protective overalls. Moreover, Raymonde demanded and obtained boots and gloves, since her own were worn out. "Kaput! Impossible to work," she said to the Major, who snapped in German, "What did I ever do to deserve such worthless women workers?"

Raymonde and her fellow workers created a newsletter to post on the walls. In it, they told about their life in the workshops and drew illustrations. They left it up during the day, but at night, Lise Ricol[72], the second-in-command of their unit, rolled it up and hid it under her straw mattress. As other deportees from Ravensbrück told me, they made tiny objects using whatever they brought back from work: bare electrical wires, pieces of fabric or leather. They used them as birthday gifts for their fellow prisoners.

A convoy of Jews wearing the yellow star arrived. Raymonde found the stars offensive and, with the help of her companions and Lise Ricol, made sure the Jews were put in their barracks.

---

[72]Lise (Ricol) London wrote her memoires, entitled, *La Mègère de la rue Daguerre. Souvenirs de Résistance.* Paris: Editions du Seuil, 1995. She mentioned the name of Charles Tillon, head of the National Military Committee and future husband of Raymonde (p. 125 and 143), but wrote nothing about Raymonde.

They then replaced their stars with red triangles marked with an "F" for French, which they stole.

American troops began to enter Germany. In Leipzig, the Germans were afraid the prisoners would be freed, so they threw them out on the road with no food, completely empty-handed. They walked for miles until they collapsed of exhaustion. After several days, they were finally able to rest in a large field. They heard the deafening noise of American bombs and realized that the SS had all disappeared. Encouraged and hopeful, they resumed their march, but in the opposite direction, towards Leipzig, which they imagined to be in the hands of the British or the Americans. They walked joyfully and enthusiastically. "We were very organized. During our occasional rest stops, we had said that if we were able to escape the column formation, we would leave in groups of five with women who spoke German. We all shook hands and said, "See you in Paris, perhaps."

Before leaving, the Germans had given them stolen coats marked with a red lead cross to keep them from escaping. Along the way, they met prisoners of war who were trying to get home. They had string, needles and scissors, so the women were able to unstitch the coats and turn them inside-out so as to hide the cross. Raymonde wanted to shorten her coat, and when she undid the hem, she heard something fall. It was a rather large diamond. She put it in her pocket and forgot about it.

In Leipzig, the women found the French repatriation mission. The Americans took them to the French troops, who gave them provisional papers. They were repatriated in cattle cars, but the conditions were far better than on the way there. "We slept on the floor, but there was straw and the main thing was to get to France. When we reached the border, many busloads of people were waiting for the deportees to pass. They showered us with packages of food, but we were unable to eat." They had to take great care with their stomachs. "We were so used to being undernourished that we had to go easy on the food."

Upon our arrival in Paris, "we heard the Marseillaise; we cried. At that moment, we did not know if we would see our families again." Raymonde and her group were taken to the Hôtel Lutetia. They gave the names of the dead people they had found in the fields and whose numbers they had been able to decipher. Raymonde finally looked in a mirror. "When I saw myself, I thought, 'No way!' We were lemon yellow in color and skinny as hell, impossible to recognize[73]. It was like watching a movie." Two days later, they all left for their native cities, promising to keep in touch.

At home, Raymonde reached into her pocket for a tissue and found the diamond in her pocket. She put it in a drawer, where it stayed for years. "It was only when my daughter was getting married that I told her fiancé I would set the diamond on her engagement ring, and that's what I did."

---

[73]J. M. Fleury had the same reaction when she saw herself in the mirror in the Hôtel Lutetia.

Interview with Henriette Kermann (June 13, 2002)

In 2002, Henriette Kermann[74] was living alone in her modest home in a suburb of Paris. At 92 years old, she was the eldest of the women Resistance fighters with whom I met.

Seventy-three years earlier, in 1931, Henriette was a member of the Amsterdam-Pleyel International Women's Committee Against War and Fascism. In 1933, she supported the Spanish Republicans. "The Resistance is not what you see in movies. They only show an ornamental Resistance."

Several years later, in 1940, Henriette was married to a trade union activist and had a four-year-old daughter. The family lived in Romainville, not far from Paris. The concierge of their building blew the whistle on Henriette's husband, and he was arrested for putting up flyers for the French Communist Party. Henriette left Romainville and moved into a hotel room in Paris, on the *Boulevard de Ménilmontant*. "At the hotel, we were treated like family. There was no formal paperwork. We paid month to month and did not worry about being traced."

After three months, her husband was freed and he went back to his regiment in Strasbourg. They were reunited in June 1940. They went to live in Paris in the hotel room Henriette had kept for them on the *Boulevard Ménilmontant*.

In October 1940, her husband found a job "in construction." He spent his evenings sabotaging German construction sites.

In November 1940, a party leader told Henriette that they needed the help of women. She immediately sprung into action.

---

[74]She wrote a short essay entitled, La *Résistance que j'ai faite, la Déportation que j'ai vécue* (FNDIRP, 2000). She died on February 7, 2007.

The party leader gave her instructions that she passed on to her husband. "Recruiting was difficult, as we could not find good Resistance fighters by going door to door. We recruited through people we knew."

Henriette put up flyers. She always took her daughter with her. "If we noticed that the flyer was crooked, we had to leave it that way. We couldn't stop. There were safety rules. We could not meet with people at metro entrances or bus stops, as there was a high risk of running into inspectors and Pétain's policemen. We also could not shake hands upon meeting. We pretended we were just strangers standing next to each other, making small talk. We were never to wait for each other nor have actual conversations."

Henriette distributed tracts. "I put them in mailboxes, but after curfew, we had to be very careful. One of our people was constantly keeping watch on the street to make sure that no one was watching us from a window. The FTP[75] bicycled around, throwing packets of tracts on the ground."

One day, a fellow Communist came to warn the Kermann family that there was to be a round-up of Jewish shop owners on the *Boulevard Ménilmontant*. The shop owners had to be alerted. "So we immediately went to tell them. We also called upon the FTP, as the two of us were not enough. We had to contact everyone, but time was running out. The round-up was scheduled for 6am the following morning. We told people, 'You cannot stay! Grab your toothbrushes and go.' Well, some of them stayed and were arrested. I saw baby carriages and children left alone." Henriette abhorred the yellow stars. When Jews went to register, she urged them not to do it, but they replied, "We do not want to

---

[75]for the partisans to keep them safe." (*La Résistance que j'ai faite, la Déportation que j'ai vécue* p.19).

break any laws." She said to them, "Law has nothing to do with it! You will be taken away."

January 1942. Henriette was spotted at a metro entrance on the *place Gambetta*. She had on her the paperwork for the place where she was going to set up her mimeograph. She had been handing out pamphlets on the steps of the metro and was on her way to meet someone with whom she would form a group. "We needed to expand the Resistance movement, as, contrary to popular belief, there were not many of us." At first she was not sure she should go to her meeting, but then changed her mind, thinking that she could blend in with the masses exiting the metro. However, the inspectors hid in the crowd. Henriette met her partner and suggested a different meeting place and time. "When I left, it seemed to me that I was being followed, but since it was merely a 10- or 11-year-old kid who stopped in front of my door, I thought, 'What's that kid doing here? I wonder why he's not out playing.' I was just a bit surprised, nothing more. I did not suspect anything." I could never have imagined that the police paid children to track people. The next morning, the police came to my place and arrested me. They searched the apartment and took me to the Judiciary Police headquarters on the *Quai des Orfèvres*, where I stayed for a week. They interrogated me the whole time, but I said nothing, not even a few words."

"Did they torture you?"

"No." In fact, they used an unconventional form of torture: sleep deprivation. They woke her up every two hours. "They wanted to get to me through attrition." As she said nothing, they planned to call her parents to bring them Henriette's daughter, who was staying with the concierge. If Henriette refused, they would make the child a ward of the state and she would never see her again.

She and her husband had agreed upon a code in advance. If something happened to one of them, and if they could make a phone call, they would say, "Go get the baby." Henriette's husband worked with her parents, who were craftsmen in Lilas, near Paris. She had to find a way to call them. Henriette's parents relied on a neighbor's phone because they did not have one. "The police asked me for the number. I hesitantly gave it to them, but I lied to them, saying that if my mother knew it was the police she would have a heart attack, since she had a weak heart. 'Tell them it's a message from me, her daughter, and that she should go get the baby. That's all; my mother will understand.' The policeman called them and my mother repeated exactly what she heard, "You need to go get the baby." My husband went right out in his blue overalls, without even washing his hands. He warned all of our group members and canceled our meetings." One of Henriette's brothers went to get her daughter, who stayed with her grandparents until the end of the war.

After her arrest, Henriette was taken to the police station, and then to the La Roquette prison. "There, we took classes. Some people learned stenography; I worked to improve my French, as I had dropped out of school at the age of 12. My father had always said school was useless." Then, she spent four days in the Fresnes prison, and from there she was sent to La Centrale in Rennes, where common law criminals were tried. "I was not tried by Germans, but by Frenchmen working for Pétain and hence for the Germans, of course. I was sentenced to five years of forced labor as a terrorist."

1944. From the Rennes prison, Henriette was taken to the Romainville fort with the other Communists. A month later, the Germans came to pick them up by bus to take them to the train station, "armed with submachine guns." From Romainville, they were deported to Ravensbrück, traveling for four days and four nights in cattle cars. "They quarantined us, supposedly to avoid illness, but we were surrounded by filth. From Ravensbrück, they sent us to Czechoslovakia."

She ended up at Zwodau, in Sudetenland, working for the Siemens factory. "As you know, all the major camps divided up the deportees according to industrial demand. They all had their specialties and Ravensbrück supplied everything for aviation. We worked on the clockwork of the V-1 missiles that they fired at London. They said, 'We need Parisian women,' because apparently we had agile hands. We were former seamstresses."

Henriette had to saw steel bars into pieces using a machine. Outraged at working for the Nazis, however, she committed sabotage. She chipped the teeth of the saw, blocking the machine. She then called the *meister* to complain about a strange noise. She created machine breakdowns every four days without ever being caught. She also worked at the cemetery *Kommando*, where she dug graves to bury the Gypsy women who had died of typhus fever.

February 1945. The Zwodau camp was about to be evacuated and Hitler had decreed that not a single deportee was to fall into Allied hands. Before leaving the camp, the head of the unit ordered the women to take off their striped dresses for disinfection. She then threw a heap of clothing on the ground and told them to help themselves. "That was when I noticed, on the pile of clothing, a solid blue work dress and a little black jacket. I realized that I could use them to escape. The SS had painted the initials "KL" (*Kamp Lager*, or "concentration camp") on our clean clothing using water-based paint."

The deportees were taken to Marienbad, Czechoslovakia. They had to be given gasoline shots. "They killed people that way, and in some camps, they took them out on the road. The SS officers had motorized vehicles and the deportees had to walk, so some of them collapsed and were shot dead."

In April 1945, on a sunlit Saturday, the deportees in their striped suits stopped in Grazlis, only to find that the city had been bombed. They kept walking and arrived in Germany, on a road that bordered a forest. "The head of the camp had left and had been replaced by a Major and several *aufseherinnen*."

The group reached a pine forest and the leader, an old SS officer, made them sit down. "In the forest, we were naturally harder to see. The SS supply wagon carrying loaves of bread and pulled along by deportees tipped over and everything fell on the ground. So all the women nearby scrambled towards it. The dogs started chasing after the bread and the deportees. The *aufsehrinnen* started hitting everyone, but the old SS officer did nothing. Pandemonium ensued."

At that moment, an idea struck Henriette. If she wanted to run, it was now or never. "I arrived in a large forest and went westward. I could hear cannon fire and I thought, 'The Allied forces are not far.' I walked all night through the forest."

She saw a stream and thought of the water-based "KL" painted on her camp dress. She had kept a piece of what had served as soap[76], and used it to rub off the label. "It was cold, so I was wearing my thick striped coat with my identification number still on it, and over it, I slipped my solid blue work dress. Then I put

---

[76]Henriette told me that the soap was really a piece of stone similar to chalk that the director of the Siemens factory had given the deportees "out of the goodness of his heart."

on the small black jacket without the "KL" and without stripes that I had found on the heap of clothing. I made a bundle out of some dead branches I had found in the woods, which served as camouflage to avoid being seen."

She met a deer, some indifferent people, a motorcycle with a sidecar and a van that had stopped to repair its engine. She hid behind a small slope. "I did not move. They left. Then I went back on the road, walking in the direction of the cannon fire. I could tell the direction I was walking by the tree trunks, which I knew were green on the northern side."

Through the trees, a man and woman on bicycles appeared, "dressed like Germans with little hats and feathers. They went the other way." Henriette hid and then started walking again at nightfall. At dawn, she arrived at a clearing. Another forest was visible in the distance. "I saw a man with a knotted cane, white gaiters, a vest with golden buttons and a small hat like *Fritz* from my books[77]. He smiled as he came towards me. He was an old man." They waved to each other and parted ways.

At the end of the road, she passed through the barbed wires in the field, reached the forest, then a town where she saw German soldiers. They were trying to hide in people's houses. A small gray Volkswagen stopped right next to her. "It's amazing how much thinking one can do in just a few seconds. It was a Corporal who had mistaken me for a peasant girl because of my bundle of twigs. He asked me something I did not understand. I put my hand up to my forehead and said the first thing that came to my mind. He took off in a flash."

---

[77]The Alsatian hero of the novel *L'Ami Fritz* by Erckmann-Chatrian, the pen name of two 19th-century French novelists. (Translator's note)

Then she met a simple soldier who gesticulated wildly as he repeated something in German. "Each time, I replied, 'Ja, ja' with a knowing air. I interpreted what he asked as 'Where are you going?' and replied, 'Frau Herman.' He signaled for me to go. I hurried to the edge of the forest. My legs were stiff and I was in a cold sweat. I was on a hilltop and in the distance, I could see vehicles moving in the dust, but they were American. I could smell the smoke of American cigarettes. Suddenly, I had wings. I was no longer walking; I was flying!"

April 17, 1945. She noticed a sentinel on a tank and introduced herself, "'Franzouz.' He did not reply, so I added, 'Paris.' Then he understood and called someone. Three soldiers arrived. One of them took me by the arm and asked me who I was. I replied that I was French and showed them my identification number." They sat Henriette down in an armchair at a table and gave her a plate with two eggs. "They had tons of them. It's amazing how many eggs the Americans eat! Their bread was so white and so light. They gave me a small box of coffee and a pack of cigarettes, but I did not smoke. They gave me something that they called cheese. I ate it, trying not to go too fast. I did not want to show that I was very hungry. I had not eaten in five days, since in the camp they only gave us water."

A Canadian soldier arrived in a jeep and questioned her in French. The next morning, they took her to headquarters to give a statement. She was to be housed at the home of the town's mayor. "They allowed me to stay in a shed in the garden, but did not let me into the house. I could not sleep." The next day, the Canadian was horrified to see that Henriette had spent the night outside. He admonished the family, who then invited the young woman for dinner. "I just drank some reconstituted bouillon and that's it. I didn't even take any bread. They took me back to the shed, but I did not want to stay there anymore." Her feet were swollen. She walked up to the gate and—oh joy!—she heard the sound of a motorcycle and then a voice cursing in French, "Oh, *merde*! It died again!"

"I realized they were Parisians. I called out to them and briefly explained my situation. They ordered me not to stay with those bastards and took me to their camp." They were S.T.O.[78] prisoners who were celebrating the liberation.

She did not want to sleep there surrounded by men, so "they built me a little shelter with wood panels, a bed frame with a wire netting and boards they covered with fern leaves. They gave me a blanket to use as a mattress. That suited me, and I stayed with them for a week."

Then the Americans came to pick her up in a truck to take her back to France. She crossed Germany with them and arrived in Kehl near the French border. From there, she took a train, traveling on the old railroad. In Metz, she was given a document that she still had in her possession on the day of our interview. "It is very tattered and has a stamp on it saying that I was repatriated. They put me on a train and took me to Paris, to the Hôtel Lutetia. It smelled bad there because all the deportees were dirty. I entered a phone booth and called my parents to ask them to pick me up." Her parents notified her husband, who rushed over with their daughter. "My daughter did not recognize me, as I had changed a great deal in three years, and so had she. Still, she knew it was me."

Thus, the adventure story has a happy ending.

---

[78]Service du Travail Obligatoire (Forced Labor).

FRENCH HEROINES, 1940-1945
Interview with Henriette Kermann (June 13, 2002)

THE "ALIBI" NETWORK
Interview with Claire Richet (June 27, 2003)

Claire Richet[79] resides in the 5th *arrondissement* of Paris. In 1939, she was living in Clermont-Ferrand[80] with her family, who had joined the Resistance. Her father taught physics and natural sciences and her mother was a school principal.

In 1940, Claire began her first year of law school. Since the beginning of the war, the University of Strasbourg and all of its campuses had taken refuge in the Auvergne region, along with two prestigious Parisian *lycées*. "This influx of students and 'eminent' professors altered the habitually peaceful lifestyle of the capital of Auvergne. The Alsatians in particular brought with them the anxiety and uneasiness generated by their proximity with Germany."

Claire refused to accept the capitulation. The students began to manifest their diagreement, primarily by printing and distributing tracts in mailboxes. Thus the Resistance, still in its infancy, took its first baby steps. Clermont-Ferrand was a mere 30 miles from Vichy, the seat of Marshall Pétain's new government, creating "a fertile climate for the young people's dissent," Claire told me.

When Claire's father, a Freemason, was "suspended" as a result of the Vichy government's decrees, things gathered speed. He lost his salary, which obliged Claire to get a job at the

---

[79]See the chapter entitled "Claire Richet. Réseau Alibi-Clermont-Ferrand" in *La France résistante* by Alain Vincennot (pp.208-213) and *Elles et Eux de la Résistance*, edited by Caroline Langlois and Michel Reynaud. Editions Tirésias, 2003.(189-193).
[80]Capital of the Auvergne region of France. (Translator's note)

Prefecture, in the driver's license department. Her mother was forced into early retirement and had to move out of her school-provided housing.

I asked, "What factors contributed to your joining the Resistance? How and why?" She exclaimed, "Coincidence, and also this sort of emotional recalcitrance we had to accepting defeat." The main motivation she cited for joining the Resistance was her family background. She added, "There was the atmosphere of being surrounded by students who had taken refuge in Auvergne, and my father's dismissal. We were just waiting for the opportunity. It presented itself, thanks to a friend who was an English teacher. He had a contact in the U.S. Embassy, which was temporarily based in Vichy. Over the course of several months, the Alibi network had been receiving political intelligence from one of the attachés of the embassy. One day, our friend brought a member of the network to our house and that was how it all started. My father gave his all to the Resistance. His knowledge of the region and his connections made it possible to obtain false papers and reliable shelters in Auvergne for Alibi's headquarters, whose cover had been blown in Spain."

The network depended on the British Intelligence Service. "We only found that out at the end of the war." It originated in Spain and around the city of Pau, France[81]. There were all sorts of intelligence; industry, factory locations, food supplies to be sent to Germany, maps of airfields, etc. The information was to be gathered all over France and relayed to London by radio. "Pools of recruitment were very diverse: railway workers, policemen, civil servants, shop owners. There were no political divisions. Affiliations were wide-ranging: Catholics, Protestants, Jews,

---

[81]The head of the network, George Charaudeau, was a native of Pau.

Socialists, right-wing people, and two priests, one of whom used the bell tower of his small rural church to conceal the radio that transmitted to London."

Claire rode her bicycle around and never carried a weapon. She conveyed a wide variety of intelligence: military information on German troop movements gleaned from railway workers, intelligence on any agricultural or industrial products leaving for Germany. She was a liaison, mainly in the Command Post near Clermont-Ferrand, which was moved frequently as a precaution. Claire was young and easily passed unnoticed. She kept her own name and never used false identity papers. "I also liaised with the Resistance movements in Auvergne, although the demands of our network were such that it was recommended to have the least possible contact with local Resistance fighters."

She was never caught, but sometimes had "delayed" fear. On October 27, 1943, her brother joined the same network and was arrested in Nîmes, where he had just obtained a map of the airfield. His family had to leave home. "My parents took refuge for a month in the southwest of France. I left for Marseille, where we were told my brother had been transferred. Our network leader hoped to 'finance' his escape. To verify that he was indeed in Marseille, I went to the Gestapo under the pretext of claiming his watch. I could have been arrested then! Fear often comes after the fact."

She described a parachuting incident. "We had chosen as a landing field for the plane sent from London, a prairie in the mountains of Rochefort. It was August, and a full moon. The small aircraft, guided by our flashlights, had dropped its containers of weapons, one of which landed in the middle of a herd. A young bull panicked and ran away. The farmers were still looking for it two days later and wrongly accusing a butcher of stealing fresh meat."

"Airdropped weapons for the use of the Maquis were transported by van at night and stowed away in an empty grave. The village mayor facilitated this because he was a friend of the network!"

Claire only had contacts on a personal level, with friends. In their network, caution was the number one rule. Only after the Liberation did members of Alibi scattered all over the regions of Bretagne, Auvergne and the Southwest of France meet. "Thanks to our rules, we had few arrests and tragedies (which were often due to carelessness). We were not to write anything down; we had to remember everything, know as little as possible about each other so as not to have anything to confess if we were arrested."

Did the Occupation change Claire? "It changed me in a very precise way. We discovered people with backgrounds extremely different from our lifestyle as civil servants in the academic field. Often, their political views were also divergent from ours. Wartime taught me a type of universalism and my friendships withstood the test of time."

Claire married Jacques Richet, a member of "Défense de la France." They had a daughter who was never really interested in their experiences. Like other Resistance fighters, Claire avowed, "Perhaps we did not feel like talking about it, concerned as we were about returning to a normal life." Grandchildren are the ones who want to know. In the past few years, some teachers have encouraged their students to become more aware of the Resistance and deportation. Former Resistance fighters are invited to tell their stories to classes. "We realized the importance of remembering and we spoke a lot to young generations, thanks to associations of former deportees or former Resistance fighters. Also, perhaps today's youth, in their search for a goal, envy us because we had an ideal: that of regaining freedom."

FRENCH HEROINES, 1940-1945
Interview with Claire Richet (June 27, 2003)

A LIFELONG COMMITMENT
Interview with Lucie Aubrac[82] *(July 5, 2001)*

The day I visited Lucie Aubrac[83] in the 13th *arrondissement* of Paris, she had just celebrated her 89th birthday. One of her former students had sent her 89 roses.

Lucie Bernard, the daughter of Burgundy winegrowers, was born in Mâcon in 1912. As a Sorbonne student, she was an activist for the groups "Etudiants pauvres" (Poor Students) and "Communist Youth." In 1936, she was a spectator at the Olympic Games in Berlin and discovered the horrors of antisemitism, which appalled her. During the civil war in Spain, she tried to join the anti-fascist side, but was rejected by the anarchists of the POUM.[84]

---

[82]Lucie Aubrac died on March 14, 2007.

[83]Her book, *Outwitting the Gestapo* (University of Nebraska Press, November 1, 1994) recounts her nine months in the Resistance concurrently with her nine months of pregnancy. The filmmaker Claude Berri made a movie adaptation entitled *Lucie Aubrac*, with actors Carole Bouquet and Daniel Auteuil in 1997. She published *Cette exigeante liberté* (L'archipel 1997), a series of interviews with Corinne Bouchoux (L'Archipel), *La Résistance expliquée à mes petits-enfants* (Seuil 2000).
Several texts mention the achievements of Lucie Aubrac, such as Simone Martin-Chauffier's *A bientôt quand même* (Calmann-Lévy, 1976). *Les Femmes dans la Résistance*, a colloquium organized by *L'union des Femmes Françaises* in November 1975, (Editions du Rocher, 1977), Ania Francos. *Il était des femmes dans la Résistance* (Stock,1978), *Elles: la Résistance*. Marie-Louise Coudert avec la collaboration de Paul Hélène (Messidor, 1983), *Pénélope. Mémoires de femmes*, réalisé par Danièle Voldman et Sylvie Van de Casteele-Schweitzer, Guylaine Guidez. *Femmes dans la guerre* 39-45 (Perrin, 1989), *Clio*, Histoire, Femmes et Sociétés No. 1, 1995. Margaret Weitz. *Sisters in Resistance: How Women Fought to Free France* (John Wiley and Sons, 1995). *Les femmes dans la Résistance en France* (colloque de 2002, Tallandier, 2003). She was interviewed on Bernard Pivot's television show, *Apostrophes*, on the theme of Rebels.

[84]Small Marxist party with revolutionary views and which included several Trotskyists.

In 1938-39, Lucie was an *Agrégée*[85] teacher of history and geography in an all-girls' high school in Strasbourg. That was where she met her future husband, Raymond Samuel, a civil engineer. He had studied for a year at MIT (Massachusetts Institute of Technology) in Boston. Lucie had won a scholarship to go to the United States and was interested in meeting Raymond, who had just come back from there. "I had to talk to him," she told me, "to learn about the country. So I looked for the guy and found him. He told me about the US, and so much more, because on May 14th, that was it: we were together forever, and that date remained very special to us." She was to leave for the US on September 5th and her luggage was already on the boat. However, war broke out on September 3rd. She could not abandon her country, her family and Raymond, who was Jewish. They were married on December 14, 1939.

She was very young, and a "passionate pacifist," as her father was a wounded veteran of World War I. She was also influenced by her professors, who spoke of racism in the United States.

During the "Phoney War," Lucie taught at the *lycée* in Vanves, a suburb of Paris. She protested against the lack of examiners and had no qualms about asking the Germans to liberate some French officers to sit on the exam juries. Her request was accepted (*Cette exigeante liberté* p. 53). She then continued to work as a *lycée* teacher in Lyon while moonlighting as a Resistance fighter.

Lucie created her own movement called *Libération*, in Strasbourg and in Clermont-Ferrand with Cavailhès, a professor of logic, and the journalist Jean d'Astier de la Vigerie. With them, she accomplished her first act of Resistance in the fall of 1940 in

---

[85]She had passed the *Agrégation*, a highly competitive examination for teachers.

Clermont-Ferrand. During the October vacation, they went to Perpignan. "We sprayed gasoline in two or three wagons with enemas that veterinarians use for animals." They thought that "Franco was sending cane sugar to the Germans and that the sugar would burn."

At the Strasbourg *lycée*, she was known as Mademoiselle Bernard, and then in Lyon[86], as Madame Lucie Samuel who had passed the prestigious *Agrégation* exam at the university. She had a very good relationship with her students, some of whose parents were collaborators. They never denounced Lucie, who was protecting two Jewish girls. Jews were not allowed to have notebooks, so Lucie asked the other students to bring needles and thread. "At the time, notebooks were just sheets of paper sewn together in the middle and with a cover. I said, 'there are two students who have no notebooks; that's not normal. Those who want to, can cut the thread, then we will take the central sheet and assemble a history and geography notebook for each of these students.' Everyone did it." Moreover, Lucie refused to take her students to see the antisemitic film, *Le Juif Süss,* despite the minister's order.

In the Resistance, Lucie took on the identity of a "single woman."

"I was a fiancée to many, because during the war, you could not use your true identity." She used the pseudonym Mademoiselle de Barbentane, which impressed people and was her ticket into the offices of authority figures. "Primped, dressed to the nines and elegant," she would let down her long, beautiful

---

[86]Lucie taught in Strasbourg and was affiliated with the University of Strasbourg. She was considered Alsatian and was transferred to Lyon when the war began in 1940.

hair and turn on the charm. "Please allow me to see my fiancé," she asked politely and respectfully. That was how she came into contact with the Gestapo.

She organized escapes. Sometimes she used subterfuge. In 1940, when Raymond was imprisoned in the *Sarre* region with other officers, she went to the barracks wearing a civilian costume and carrying a gift for the sentry. She was thus able to see Raymond and give him a substance that provoked a high fever. That evening, he ended up in the hospital. "At that time, the Germans had access to the Red Cross, and the sick were taken to the hospital. There were no major prison camps yet." Lucie entered her husband's room with blue work overalls hidden under her dress. She put them under his blanket, and that night, Raymond scaled the wall and was met on the other side by the Resistance fighters from his independent group. Lucie and Raymond went back to France.

Sometimes, Lucie threatened her adversary to obtain what she wanted. To illustrate this, she gave me the example of how the Resistance fighters fled from St. Etienne in 1943. In order to find the prisoners' unit, she put on a white robe and stethoscope, and wandered the hallways for a week pretending to be a nurse. "Starting in the fall of '42, I headed a special group in charge of evasions in the secret army of the Resistance. In my book, moreover, I tell about the breakout of four Resistance fighters in St. Etienne. It was just my job, nothing more. Of course, I was primarily assigned to setting up escapes involving Raymond. And that time, since he was arrested by the French police, one would have thought it would be easier." Raymond was to be released on

May 24th, but our magic date was the 14th[87]. So Lucie went to see the prosecutor and ordered him to sign Raymond's temporary release for May 14th, otherwise "you will not see the sun set on the evening of the 14th," she told him with great conviction. He signed it.

Lucie had a baby boy and was expecting her second child. She often played the role of a pregnant woman. At the beginning of her pregnancy, she used a pillow to look more pregnant. When she took the train in Mâcon to cross the demarcation line, she told the railway workers who questioned her, "'Oh, I want to see my husband because I have not heard from him in a long time, and I don't feel well with my baby coming in two months!' The guys let me through every time. That's how deception works. I think that's what young people need to understand. It's not heroism. You need to use your skills."

As we spoke, Lucie emphasized to me the crucial role and importance of women in the Resistance. They can play the lovelorn one, the charmer, the seducer: "I get very annoyed when people say that women did not fight. They fought with their feminine weapons, using seduction. The Red Cross was made up of women; they were the ones who took packages to prisons. Who went there to pick up the dirty laundry and bring it back washed? Women." She cites the example of Emmanuelle, who brought shirts one day, with a message rolled up in the hem of one of them. The Gestapo caught her. "The German woman beat her, rolled her on the ground, tore out her hair. She was 19 years old. She died at Ravensbrück. That's Resistance, not rifles or grenades."

---

[87]Lucie and Raymond had vowed to always be together on May 14th, the anniversary of the day they fell in love. They always succeeded, except on May 14, 1944, when Raymond was in Algiers with General de Gaulle.

If a parachutist landed on a police station and broke his leg, a woman Resistance fighter picked him up in her car. When they were stopped for inspection, she would say she was taking a wounded man to the hospital. It seemed perfectly normal and the inspector would let them pass."

Lucie's incredible feat was organizing Raymond's escape from the Montluc prison in Lyon[88]. It took several months of preparations and "this escape could only be facilitated by a woman," she told me. Lucie went to see the Gestapo under the name of Ghislaine de Barbentane, an heiress living in the *Château Duplessis* in the *Saône et Loire* region. Her request was a serious one: she claimed to be unmarried and carrying a prisoner's baby. She did not ask for his liberation, but simply the right to marry him to save her honor. As a single mother, she would automatically be ostracized by her family and society. She wanted to avoid humiliation. "The German who saw me every week had done his research. Mademoiselle de Barbentane existed. He did not think for a moment that I was someone else. An heiress who is unmarried and pregnant, you can imagine!"

Lucie was harshly turned away from the Montluc prison by Barbie, but she did not give in[89]. She went to see "Pierre of the false papers," a Resistance fighter from her independent group whose friend knew a German Colonel. That friend helped Lucie get in to see the German Colonel, recommending that she bring him a gift to make things go smoother. Taking along a box of cognac, Lucie went to see the Colonel, who had a friend in the

---

[88]This was after his arrest on June 21, 1943, in Caluire with Jean Moulin at the home of Dr. Dugoujon (*Outwitting the Gestapo*).

[89]Some of the Resistance fighters with whom I spoke affirmed that it was impossible to leave Montluc once one was inside. They had doubts about Lucie Aubrac's visits.

Gestapo. She feigned innocence and used her feminine wiles to beguile the officer, describing her weakness, her passion for the prisoner, her suffering and her pregnancy. Marriage was her only hope, she insisted, plying him with gifts. She came back time and time again until the day she discovered the French law on "marriage in extremis," which allowed a criminal condemned to death to marry, thus giving a legitimate name to his child. Lucie had to meet with Raymond and have him consent to this marriage. Her husband's first reaction was pretending not to know her, but then he understood her stratagem. Then there was the signing of the marriage contract. Lucie found a notary who was "scared stiff" of entering the prison, but agreed. The day of the signature arrived. She barely spoke to Raymond, who gave her a wink of complicity. She went to publish the marriage banns.

Lucie wanted to hurry things along, so she looked for a way to get Raymond another medication that would make him ill. He would then be transported to the hospital, whence escaping would be easier. A doctor friend suggested injecting formic acid into a piece of soap to give Raymond a rash. Unluckily, however, "my poor husband received the package and when he saw this horrid-looking soap, he thought it must be something to make him sick, so he ate it!" Lucie continued to work on her husband's liberation with her independent group. The next step was attacking the prison van taking Raymond to his interrogation. The first attempt failed.

Lucie left for Switzerland to buy "silencers" to kill the guards. The second escape attempt was a success; the guards were shot. Raymond, along with the prisoner he was handcuffed to, jumped. He was wounded and taken to a hiding place Lucie had prepared.

They were finally reunited and ended up fleeing to England[90]. Lucie, about to give birth to their second child, took laudanum to delay her delivery. Her daughter Catherine was born during the night of February 11th to 12th.

Impressed by her boldness, I exclaimed to Mrs. Aubrac, "What courage! What nerve!" She responded, "Yes, a lot more nerve than courage. Today, of course, you know all about the Gestapo's methods, the concentration camps, the genocide, the death trains, torture, waterboarding and all that. But at the time, we did not know. My commitment to the Resistance was voluntary. I had decided that I would participate with other university students in fighting against the Nazis and the Vichy collaboration. When you are a volunteer, you cannot chicken out. You are fighting because you want to gain back freedom, because you cannot accept that a Communist, a trade unionist, a Jew, or a foreigner is arrested simply because he is a Communist, trade unionist, Jew or foreigner. You cannot accept it. So you fight. But I think that what I did was not heroism; it was skill. I worked hard to use my feminine wiles."

After the war, Lucie first became a member of parliament, but she preferred not to pursue a career in politics. She went back to teaching, her true passion. She left Paris in 1952 to go live in a suburb, where she settled with her large family in a spacious home surrounded by a garden. "We had three children and we were raising five, because we had an agreement with the Resistance movement: if a couple disappeared, we had to raise their children."

---

[90]For more details, read *Outwitting the Gestapo*, which describes in detail Raymond's ultimate evasion, their departure for England and the birth of their daughter.

FRENCH HEROINES, 1940-1945
Interview with Lucie Aubrac (July 5, 2001)

Despite all her personal and professional obligations, Lucie continued to fight for peace and justice, and against racism. She was Vice President of the League for Human Rights. In 1970, she testified against Klaus Barbie and has unrelentingly denounced human barbarism in all her speeches ever since. In 2005, the television channel *France 3* showed a film made by a filmmaker from Québec, in which Lucie told her life story. The film showed her visits to schools, where she encouraged young people to fight against injustice. One could sense that Lucie Aubrac was at ease with students. She was very relaxed and made them laugh. Nevertheless, the schoolchildren were speechless with admiration for the heroine.

FRENCH HEROINES, 1940-1945
Interview with Lucie Aubrac (July 5, 2001)

A CIVIC DUTY
Interview with Noëlla Rouget (July 11, 2002)

In 1940, Noëlla was a boarding school teacher in Angers. She distributed tracts along with the students. She learned to type using a textbook she bought, printed and mimeographed leaflets, and distributed underground newspapers such as *Défense de la France* , *Combat* , *Témoignage Chrétien*. She became a liaison, carrying letters or suitcases, whose contents were never revealed to her, to predetermined receiving points. She only found out after the war that she had been part of a local network called *"Honneur et Patrie,"* (Honor and Fatherland).

One day, several of her peers were arrested. One of them fled, and his parents were arrested in his place. "In order to avoid the risk of that happening to my parents, I remained where I was on June 23rd, 1943, when the Gestapo came to our apartment to check if we were tuned in to the BBC in London. They also searched the house but found nothing. They took me to their headquarters for a 'simple questioning,' they said." She was to be married in three weeks and she did not know that her fiancé, a major Resistance fighter, would be arrested and shot in December 1943. The inspectors asked Noëlla's brother, a priest, to come with them. "Reverend, since you are a priest, you know that lying is a sin." They questioned him and he was released after midnight. Noëlla, however, was beaten and imprisoned. "Around 1 a.m., they took me to the Angers prison, in a car with two men and a dog. The next day, they undressed me and took all the jewelry I cherished." Every morning, the Gestapo came to ask her if she was ready to talk. Each time, she replied that she had nothing to say. She stayed for three weeks, wearing her only light summer dress, her whereabouts "absolutely confidential," with nothing at all—not a book, not a paper, not a pencil. "It made me sad to think how distressed my parents were, especially my mother."

The food was always the same: a clear broth in which floated "a handful of stringy green beans" and dry bread. "Luckily, after three weeks, we were allowed to receive packages from our parents with food and a change of clothing." She refused to sleep on the straw mat and kept her clothes on at night. Her brother offered to take her place, but the Gestapo would not let him.

Like other prisoners, she communicated with the women in neighboring cells by tapping out letters of the alphabet on the wall to make words. "It is extraordinary how nimble one can get after a while. We were able to have real conversations. I found out, for example, that my neighbor was a woman to whom I had brought a suitcase once, without knowing what was inside. It had contained weapons!" Noëlla's neighbor also gave her one of the pencil leads that her parents had sent her in a package. She wrapped it in a scrap of paper and threw it in the courtyard where they went "for air" every once in a while. "I was thus able to reassure my parents by sending them a message rolled up in the hem of a skirt. I always said that all was well, even if that was not true. That made me feel less isolated in the prison. Three months later, they gave me a cellmate. At the beginning, I avoided her like the plague because I thought she was there to get information out of me. But it turned out she was a nice woman. She was from Angers as well."

The furniture in their cell consisted of a table and a stool attached to the floor by metal angle brackets. Noëlla and her cellmate, Yvette, managed to unscrew the stool and balance it precariously on the edge of the baseboard. "So we could reach the casement window, which was very high. It was always open and thus we asked our fellow prisoners who received newspapers in their packages, or whose cells faced the street, for news of the war."

Alas, one day, an SS officer unexpectedly opened the door to find Noëlla perched on the stool and Yvette standing on the box with a hole in it that served as a toilet. Neither one of them moved. They were punished: the stool was taken away from them and they were deprived of bread for three days. Luckily, Noëlla's parents had sent her some crackers that she kept hidden. She shared them with her cellmate.

She was transferred to Compiègne with the prisoners who were to be sent to Germany. "We were crowded in with common-law prisoners: prostitutes who had infected German soldiers and women black marketeers." Noëlla finally got some fresh air. After being in prison, Compiègne felt like "freedom." The women were all together and they could talk to each other.

Very soon, Noëlla was assigned to the big deportation convoy, "the convoy of thousands." "That was when I became friends with Geneviève de Gaulle." They traveled for three days and three nights. "We remained locked in cattle cars." The conditions were humiliating. "We had a big vat made of sheet metal to use as a toilet. During a brief stop in Germany, they made us get out to empty it. We had to relieve ourselves in a trench in the ground, in front of all the people who were waiting on the train platform." When they arrived, SS men and women, with their ferocious dogs at their side, threw open the doors. They violently pulled out the deportees, beating them with their canes. "We were exhausted, aching and dazzled."

They finally reached Fürstenberg, and then Ravensbrück[91] after an arduous and exhausting walk. "It was the dead of night. Our entrance was very theatrical. There were bright projectors, armed SS men on one side and women with threatening dogs on the other." They waited for a long time in the cold, until wake-up time in the camp, 3:30 a.m. The first group of women entered the showers and came out unrecognizable. Noëlla stared at them with horror. "They were dressed like convicts, in blue and gray stripes, with shaven heads. Then it was our turn, and we went in with great trepidation. After the showers, we were once again crowded into living quarters. There were approximately a thousand of us women. We thought, optimistically, that they were sending us to work in the camps in Germany as punishment for having committed acts against Nazism."

Noëlla was in quarantine for several days. Her food consisted of a ladleful of blackish brew made of acorns, morning and evening. At lunchtime, she received a ladleful of clear liquid in which swam three or four pieces of woody rutabagas, and in the evening, "a tiny slice of bread."

She was assigned to Unit 27, one of the most unpleasant ones, because it also contained common law prisoners and prostitutes. She and her friends had to hide their scarce possessions, even their bowls, so they would not be stolen. "Without bowls, we would not have been able to eat. After twelve hours of work[92], utterly

---

[91]All of the women sent to the Ravensbrück camp describe it the way Noëlla does. Their work earned a lot of money for Himmler, who owned the camp.

[92]Thierrar, the Minister of Justice, had said about those who were to be eliminated: Jews, Gypsies and enemies, "there is nothing better than work and that work must be exhausting in the exact meaning of the word."

exhausted, we had to sleep four to a bed, with our knees touching, on 3-level bunks with straw mattresses 25 inches wide."[93]

She had fleas. "In the evening, if we had the energy and light, we had to 'de-flea' ourselves. Throughout my entire captivity, I wore the same shirt and pants. They had been disinfected, but not washed and they were blood-stained."

The siren sounded at 3:30 a.m., the time when blood pressure and the temperature were at their lowest. They had to get up quickly, gulp down their so-called "coffee", and then there was the bathroom rush. The toilets were smeared with excrement and no longer had doors. "We had no paper, nor towels, nor soap. There were ten toilets and twenty sinks for 1000 women. We had to do everything at record speed because at 4am we had to be ready for the terrible 'zählappels'. There were, at times, over 38,000 of us women in the camp. So, counting everyone without errors was very difficult. We had to be in front of our unit, lined up perfectly, standing in groups of ten side by side. Helping a woman who had fainted was strictly forbidden! We had to hold up that way for two or three hours, in any weather, in the snow, wind and rain. If it was raining, our dresses remained wet for days and days, as we had no way of drying them."

The prisoners worked in various "work columns": wood, coal, painting or roads. Noëlla was assigned to the forest column, which entailed digging huge trenches around trees that had been sawed down by the SS. They had to unearth the tree trunk and dig a 30-foot-long trench using ineffective tools. "As always, when we did not work fast enough, they beat us." The advantage of this kind of work was being in the open air, a vast improvement over

---

[93]Smaller than a twin bed. (translator's note)

the tall, confining walls of Ravensbrück. Noëlla "organized"[94] wood coal to bring back for her sick friends. Moreover, she sometimes found something to eat in the forest. "We were so famished that we would eat acacia leaves or grass."

The work was draining. Later, she was placed in the group of *Verfügbar,* (the available ones). She worked in every sector, but luckily not in the war industry. When she had to dig with a shovel, she tried to work more slowly. "The *aufseherinnen* were constantly near us. They hit us if the shovel was not full enough or if our pace was too slow."

"Noëlla Rouget, how did you manage to hold up?" The heroine's reply resembled that of all the other heroines. "Solidarity saved us. We cheered up those whose morale was flagging. We did things for each other that were small but invaluable: touching the shoulder of a friend who was in bad shape during the awful morning roll calls, or rub the back of the woman standing in front of us when the *aufseherinnen* were not looking. They would quickly throw a bucket of ice water on any woman unfortunate enough to faint. Some of my fellow prisoners even managed to save up some of their bread to bake a cake for a birthday. That may seem laughable today, but for us, this treat was a great source of comfort."

During her internment, Noëlla had typhus fever and pleurisy. She fainted and was transported to the *revier*, or infirmary, which all the deportees hated. In 1942 and '43, the women sent there would disappear. "I received no treatment, but I got out alive." One day, the camp personnel came to get those who could walk. A nurse roused Noëlla and announced to the SS guard that she was perfectly capable of working. "I did not feel capable at all and

---

[94]In the camp jargon, "organize" meant "steal."

I was on the verge of tears." The nurse was from the *Sarre* province of Germany which had formerly belonged to France. "Perhaps that was why she took pity on me and saved my life, since the next day I found out that those who had remained in the infirmary had been gassed."

In October 1944, Himmler, the head of the camp, declared, "There are not enough deaths at Ravensbrück. Eliminate 2000 more women per month." Those who were ill in the *revier* died after having been forced to swallow a white powder. The deportees who worked in the paint column had to empty all the drums of paint and make a hole in the ceiling. They realized that they were preparing a gas chamber. "Every evening, we were terrified." Himmler tried to convince General de Gaulle to exchange members of his family for German hostages. When the General refused, Himmler turned to the International Red Cross. Through the intermediary of Count Bernadotte, a cousin of the King of Sweden, Noëlla was part of the first prisoner exchange which took place on April 4, 1945. She was among 300 Frenchwomen handed over to the Swiss authorities, who then transported them to France.

She came home, but she had tuberculosis. Geneviève de Gaulle suggested she go to Switzerland, where the mountain air would do her good. Indeed, she recovered and even met her future husband. She now lives in Geneva and has two sons and two grandchildren. "That is a victory over Nazism!"

The years of war altered many of her youthful opinions. I was raised in a Catholic environment, where right-wing was white and left-wing was black. Yet, I saw people on the right who did not always act properly and vice versa. I met Communists, such as Marie-Claude Vaillant Couturier, an exemplary woman, who, in

'45, preferred to stay in the camp until July to help the bedridden instead of leaving when she could." The truth, or rather, the reality, was somewhere in a gray zone far from the two extremes. Noëlla ended up realizing that one cannot put people in categories to judge them. "I was scandalized when we first arrived in Compiègne: there were prostitutes among us. One of them accidentally bumped into me and addressed me in an informal manner. I had come from an upscale boarding school, where we were expelled for addressing people that way. But I quickly changed. With the war and the Resistance, my universe shifted. I saw things in a totally different perspective from the one my education had given me."

Noëlla suffered for a long time from the repercussions of tuberculosis and experienced several depressions. Feeling tired and misunderstood, she did not want to write her memoirs. Upon her return to Paris, a woman asked her if they had given her food in the camp. She replied that they had been starving. The woman retorted, "But we were starving, too, Madame."

"So I realized that words did not have the same depth of meaning for these people as they did for us, and that made me lose my desire to talk about it."

Noëlla has always been modest when talking about her activities as a Resistance fighter to her grandchildren. "I'm sure they know much less about me than the students I speak to in schools. I have to admit that the nightmares that haunted me for a very long time disappeared as soon as I told the students about my experiences."[95]

---

[95]Noëlla, whom I recently spoke with, told me she accompanied some young people to Auschwitz in 2006, and had done so twice before that.

FRENCH HEROINES, 1940-1945
Interview with Noëlla Rouget (July 11, 2002)

One day in Geneva, Noëlla was interviewed by journalists who still doubted the existence of gas chambers at Ravensbrück. She exclaimed to these revisionists,[96] "They did exist, since our Major recognized that they did! He even told about the gassing he had witnessed. That is why I decided to speak in schools." And she told them, "There is only one race: the human race."

---

[96]The "Revisionists" are a few people who, for various reasons, vehemently deny the existence of the genocide of Jews during the Second World War.

FRENCH HEROINES, 1940-1945
Interview with Noëlla Rouget (July 11, 2002)

ONCE A FIGHTER, ALWAYS A FIGHTER
Interview with Marie-Jo Chombart de Lauwe
(July 8, 2002)

At the outset of the war, Marie-Jo was in her second-to-last year of school in Tréguier, near the northern coast of Brittany. Her parents were in their summer home on the Ile de Bréhat, off the coast of Brittany. When Nazi troops occupied Brittany, Marie-Jo went to stay with her parents.

"It was the perfect place for my activities, as I was able to help hidden British fighters. The example of my patriotic family helped me find the courage to join the Resistance. One of my grandfathers, a Belgian, had lived in Poland. He had written a book called *Les Héroïnes*, about Polish women who had rebelled against the tzar's army. My mother had enlisted as a nurse on the front in World War I, and my father was a wounded World War I veteran."

Marie-Jo drew the Cross of Lorraine[97] and the victory V on walls. When she went out, she always made sure to wear France's colors: blue, white and red. In 1940, she was seventeen years old. The Resistance movement asked her to bring an Englishman to Bréhat island. "They had put a beret on him to make him look somewhat French and he had a fake identity card with a French name. My mother, who worked at the City Hall, had obtained it for him. We had to take a boat. A German soldier who checked everyone's ID sat in a sentry box a bit further on. The Englishman and I arrived on our bicycles. To get on the boat, of course, we had to get off our bikes. Just as I was about to do so, the Englishman

---

[97]See translator's note p. 86 (interview with J.M. Fleury).

gallantly picked up the front wheel of my bike, and the young German sentry took the back wheel, and they carried my bike down together." Marie-Jo and the Englishman reached their destination without a hindrance.

Marie-Jo worked with her mother, who was the coordinator of a group called, "La bande à Sidonie (Sidonie's Crew)." In order to communicate directly with London, the two women gave some men a letter saying, "Send us someone so we can have a permanent channel of communication." Shortly afterwards, a British agent came by boat from London to the Ile de Bréhat. He assisted in organizing a network, which included two groups: those in charge of continuing to aid in escapes, based in the villages of Paimpol and Plouha, and those in charge of gathering intelligence. The first group continued to hide British pilots, for example. "When we could, we went to get them, hid them and helped them to leave when the time came." Marie-Jo and her team were part of the second group: "We were in charge of sending information to London."

At age 18, having passed her *baccalauréat* (high school graduation examination), Marie-Jo spent the summer bicycling all over the Brittany coast and picking up defense maps drawn by their agents. In the fall, she went to medical school in the city of Rennes. There, she joined the heads of her Franco-English network, "31 George France," whose leader was an engineer working at the train station.

"This allowed him to have all the information regarding the schedules of German trains carrying weapons. A secretary and interpreter communicated with the German transportation office, and he brought the information. It was a key position. In Rennes, there was also a hidden radio operator who coded and transmitted

FRENCH HEROINES, 1940-1945
Interview with Marie-Jo Chombart de Lauwe (July 8, 2002)

information that could quickly be sent to London." Rennes, the capital of Brittany, was simply an occupied zone, whereas the entire coast was a no-access zone. Marie-Jo managed to obtain a pass, ostensibly because she needed to see her parents.

"I regularly made trips to Saint-Brieuc on the coast, where my grandmother still lived and where my mother brought the maps. Or I went to the Ile de Bréhat and brought back documents to Rennes. I often met with the interpreter in a cafe there. He gathered what I brought him and sent it to London by sea." When there was urgent information, Marie-Jo received an ordinary letter from her mother. She heated it to see the message written in lemon juice, which functioned as invisible ink, and she took it to the radio to transmit.

Sometimes the Royal Air Force attacked the area. They tried to destroy German aircraft on the ground leaving for Great Britain. The Germans then sought out contractors to repair the aircraft. "Our agents were the ones who came as contractors." They saw the types of weapons the Germans had, and sometimes they were even able to enter the offices. The intelligence thus obtained was invaluable for the British.

However, the German counter-intelligence agencies were on the lookout, trying to infiltrate the French Resistance movement. Those in charge of escapes were the first to be arrested, and after them, the three main agents in Rennes. "We were worried and we no longer had a link to London. We searched for one through another group that was in charge of weapons airdrops, but it had already been infiltrated by a double agent, Roger Diebolt. He started working with us and contacted all the people on the coast, including myself and another student who worked with me. Diebolt gave all the intelligence and evidence against all of us to the counter-intelligence agency. On May 22, 1942, we were all arrested at the same time in several locations along the coast."

Marie-Jo was housed in a student dormitory room in Rennes. The doorbell rang early in the morning. She opened the door and naively asked, "What's the problem?"

"You are under arrest!"

"I innocently asked, 'Oh! Why?' and they replied, 'You know all too well.' They told me to get dressed, I closed the door and got into the black car. That was the cutoff point. I felt like an iron curtain had closed off my past from my future. I had passed into the other side of life."

She was nineteen years old. What did the future hold for her? She did not lose courage nor hope. "When a Resistance fighter was arrested, that did not mean we stopped resisting. We tried to continue to fight: standing up to questioning, trying to gather information and whatever else we could do."

After her arrest, she was taken to the Kommandantur, where her papers were taken from her, and then to the Rennes prison. The next day, as she sadly entered the prison lobby, she saw her thirteen colleagues and both her parents. She quickly realized who had betrayed them. She was transferred to the big military prison in Angers, where she remained "in a secret location" for several weeks.

The interrogations began "in a sort of cellar." She noticed the defense maps spread out on the table and thought, "A death sentence for espionage is a sure thing with these maps as evidence." A man in black surrounded by several soldiers questioned her: "Why were you arrested? She replied, "I should ask you that. Why did you arrest me?" He retorted, "We ask the questions here, not you, and in any case, we have all the proof."

FRENCH HEROINES, 1940-1945
Interview with Marie-Jo Chombart de Lauwe (July 8, 2002)

At the beginning, she had received instructions to deny the evidence, so she continued to repeat, "I don't know what that is."

Was she tortured? "No, but I was threatened all the time, beaten and they put me in a cell at the end of the men's row. I only had a straw mat and except for stale bread, I was deprived of food for several days. I was not afraid; I held up. I still had the full Resistance mindset." The questioning continued. The inspectors even tried to blackmail her. "Your father is a World War I veteran with a medal. If you come and work for us, we will release him."

They told her that her mother had admitted everything. "I said that my mother did not speak a word of German, and he exclaimed that he had signed along with her to guarantee the authenticity of her deposition. I replied, 'Your signature means nothing to me.' He confronted me with my mother who, with a wink, explained to me 'Things seem worse than they actually are; tell them we found the maps.' It was a delay tactic."

Marie-Jo carved the words "Honneur et Patrie" on the walls of the prison in Angers. When she went "for walks" or to questionings, she was always accompanied by soldiers, but she tried to linger in the stairwells, thinking of a way to see her fellow group members. "I wanted to communicate with the men from our group who were in neighboring cells, but how? I no longer had a chair or a table, but there was a casement window at the top with broken glass. When you're idle 24 hours a day, you become very creative. I found tiny bits of string in my straw mat, which I knotted together to make a rope. I rolled up my mat and got on top of it and slipped the rope between two bars. One day, I was caught. The furious Major pulled my hair, saying, 'If you continue this, I will put you in a dark cell with no food, with rats!' I retorted, 'Then I'll eat the rats.'"

A few of the soldiers proved to Marie-Jo that their hearts were not made of stone. She remembers the compassion of one of them, who said, "Women in prison, how sad. I'm not a mean guy. If my colleague comes, I'll yell out '22'."

"When that guard watched over the prisoners in the tiny, isolated individual courtyards, he would come and get me even when I did not have the right to go out. Another guard, a young Polish soldier whose punishment was to work in the prison for a time, served soup and was not supposed to give me any. But at the end of meal distribution, he opened my cell window and gave me a jar of honey he had stolen from the cafeteria." He was a *"malgré nous"* soldier, forced to serve in the army against his will.

Marie-Jo stayed in the Angers prison for two and a half months. Then she was transferred to the Santé prison. She was the only one in the requisitioned train compartment, "between two German *Feldgendarmes*." The prison was infested with bed bugs and rats. Marie-Jo was once again "in a secret location." Some prisoners were awaiting execution. She wondered if she would be next. She tapped on the walls, forming words out of letters of the alphabet. She also communicated through the casement window. That was how she met Marie-Claude Vaillant-Couturier[98] and France Bloch Sérazin[99]. She also used "another, much better form of communication," which the group called, "the telephone." They spoke to each other through the toilet seats, which were directly connected to the sewers. "I will always remember the most beautiful, grandest aspect of human beings: courage and simplicity." She never complained. On the contrary, she had

---

[98]Marie-Claude Vaillant-Couturier made her name as a Commnist member of Parliament after the war.

[99]This young chemist, Jewish and Communist, was deported and decapitated in Hamburg in February 1943.

amazing endurance and an extremely positive attitude. "In this ice-cold world where death reigned, I also discovered an incredible vitality which prevailed, and that's where I met some remarkable people."

From the squalid Santé prison, she was sent to the slightly cleaner one in Fresnes. She underwent psychologically probing interrogations at the Gestapo headquarters on *rue des Saussaies*. At her last questioning, she was told, "There's no point in making you sign; you lie all the time." They proceeded to classify her N.N. (*"Nacht und Nebel"*).[100] She resumed her risky escapade with the casement window, which she opened using an iron bar from the metal base of her bed as a screwdriver. She was caught and placed in solitary confinement once again, in a "secret location." She was subjected to a total of nine months of isolation in the three prisons.

In July 1943, Marie-Jo was deported to Ravensbrück in a convoy of 58 women labeled N.N. Upon their arrival they were greeted by scrawny creatures with shaved heads and wearing rags. They could not believe that these women were from the camp. "That's impossible; there must be a penal colony nearby." However, they had no time to reflect upon the issue. "We were immediately taken to the showers, and they took everything from us. If a woman had a wedding ring, they yanked it off; they even searched our private parts. We became simply numbers in uniforms. Mine was 21,706, and they put us to work."

A day in Ravensbrück entailed a race for the cold water faucets, a rush to drink the abominable "coffee," the endless roll call, rain or shine, and twelve-hour work days. "I toiled in a sandpit. We had to dig and pile shovelfuls of sand up on top,

---

[100]The deportees labeled "Darkness of Night" were to disappear without a trace.

where there were wagons on tracks that we had to fill. Then I worked on roads. We placed the clinker and there were scoria to level on the ground. Today, there are mechanical steamrollers, but back then, they were pulled by women." The labor was exhausting and naturally, if they did not go fast enough, they were beaten.

Afterwards, Marie-Jo was "hired" by the Siemens factory. She assembled electrical parts. With the help of her fellow workers, she strove to block the machines. They wanted to slow down production. To remain human, as several of them told me, they made small gifts for each other. Marie-Jo used the tools of her meticulous work to sculpt her humble offerings. She explained, "In that awful world, we had to try to keep up our spirits, continue to resist and remain rational human beings."

For lunch, there was cabbage and rutabaga soup. In the evening, they received a piece of bread, a small cube of margarine or a tiny slice of sausage. After curfew, the deportees lay down, sleeping "two, then three to a bed, squeezed like sardines, with lots of parasites: there were lice and fleas that made us itch. We also had scabies. If we had scratches or wounds, they did not heal because we were malnourished. We became very skinny. We were in a dreadful physical state."

On Sundays, despite the chores, the prisoners tried to meet in small groups behind the barracks. "We talked; we had formed a chorus, and teachers recited poems." Marie-Jo had established some rules to keep their dignity and remain strong: Never become demoralized; never listen to your inner voice complain; speak to yourself harshly, and most importantly, always wash. In these slummy conditions, cleanliness was key. "I tried to go and wash up before the first morning roll call. I realized that if you had the strength and were healthy enough to splash yourself with cold water, you did not feel the cold as much afterwards."

"Genocide," Marie-Jo told me, "is the worst of crimes against humanity; it is an absolute evil." Entire convoys of men, women and children were sent to the gas chambers. Atrocious medical experiments were performed on mostly Polish girls, used as "guinea pigs." The Nazi doctors cut out pieces of their bones and muscles. They sterilized little Gypsy girls with liquid introduced through their genitals to burn their fallopian tubes.

What affected Marie-Jo most was her work in the "children's room." Babies were born in Ravensbrück, but they could not survive. There was no milk, no diapers or clothing. Marie-Jo brainstormed actively to find solutions. She and the other women worked together and enlisted the help of all the women in the camp. "We had some linens from the women who worked in fabric workshops. For food, we received one jar of milk per day and two baby bottles. That was not enough for thirty or forty children, so thank goodness for cooperation! The women who worked in the kitchen found us ten small bottles."

How could they get the babies to drink? They had to be very inventive. One of the prisoner nurses stole a pair of rubber gloves from the central infirmary and they used the fingers to make nipples for bottles. It was not very hygienic; babies got infected, and actually, "there were very few survivors despite all our efforts. Every day a child died, then two, then three... You can imagine the mothers' grief when they came to feed the children. They themselves had run out of milk."

Worst of all, Marie-Jo told me, was that after these babies died, the death had to be declared and they had to be taken to the morgue, which was in front of the crematorium. Marie-Jo described that room, which was a symbol of the Nazi terror and their contempt for life. "It was the most awful picture I had ever seen when I went down there for the first time. I turned on the light and there was a pile of dead bodies thrown every which way, with wide open eyes and mouths. It was the scream of death. I saw frozen dead women with dark red and black legs, and women with their stomachs cut open. Nazi medical students had practiced cesarian sections on them. Ripped-out gold teeth were lying on a table. I had entered death's den, holding in my arms babies that I had grown fond of and that I had to leave there. It was absolutely atrocious. I could not bring myself to leave those babies in that horrible heap. In the end, I put them in the arms of one of the least grotesque women's bodies. But all of that is indescribable."

After her internment at Ravensbrück, Marie-Jo was sent to Mauthausen, in Austria, with 1,900 other prisoners. "It was the 'black convoy,' or the convoy of people with the worst image." The trip took five days. They only received enough bread for three days. After an exhausting voyage, they arrived at night at the Mauthausen train station and had to walk to their new camp, three miles "uphill." The women who could not go on simply collapsed and were killed. Marie-Jo feared that her 54-year-old mother would not make it. Luckily, Marie-Jo's determination won out and she supported her mother to the end of the long walk.

However, Marie-Jo's anxiety increased when they reached their destination. It was a men's camp and the women feared the worst. They were searched in the nude by the male prisoners. Luckily, the latter were very decent and just as humiliated as the women, whom they had to scrutinize for body lice.

The rest of the time, the women and men were separated. The weakest ones were sent to another camp in the north, in

Bergen-Belsen. The others were quickly put to work. "We worked twelve hours in a sorting station called Amsteten, which had been bombed by US Army planes. We had to clear away the wreckage, lift up train tracks, which was exhausting for us poor women. We were supervised by young, very brutal soldiers who had been indoctrinated since the age of ten in the '*Hitler Jugend*,' like all young Germans." They slept on the floor in an empty factory, drank water from a small stream and had a bucket to use as a toilet.

On April 22, 1945, the deportation was over for Marie-Jo and her mother. The International Red Cross, through the intermediary of Count Bernadotte, finally liberated them. They were sent back by truck to Switzerland, where they received medical care. Then they traveled to Paris, and finally to St. Brieuc, where they were met by Marie-Jo's grandmother and two sisters. They all left for Bréhat island. The Mayor, "with his blue, white and red band and the schoolchildren with lots of bouquets" welcomed them. The Mayor gave a speech they found touching, but nowhere near the infernal reality they had lived through. Marie-Jo was extremely tired, and back in a world she no longer understood. She was sad to learn of her father's death at Buchenwald.

She was 22 years old. Thanks to a small "allowance" she received as a member of the "military," she spent several months writing all the notes that later formed her book[101]. She married Paul-Henri Chombart de Lauwe, who encouraged her to take courses. She specialized in social studies. She recovered gradually, but was invaded by fear when she was pregnant with her first child. "I felt an irrepressible anxiety when I remembered

---

[101] *Toute une vie de résistance.* Editions Graphein, 1998.

that for several months, I began each day with dead children. I gave birth to a beautiful little girl, and then I had a second girl and two boys."

Marie-Jo ended our interview with these words: "I have a wish that we keep memory alive as time passes, as the deportees are disappearing and there are also revisionists who deny what happened. Nazism is not over. The ideology inspired a political party, and when that happens, everything is under its control: the army, the police, the justice system and concentration camps. We must talk about it, tell people how far it can all go. That is how and why we must continue, so that young people know."

MY GRANDMOTHER RIVKA LEIBA

I wish that I had had more time to get to know my 61-year-old grandmother, who saved her son and oldest granddaughter. She hastily sent me into hiding by train on August 24th, 1942, with no time to write my name for identification. But even without a nametag, I was welcomed by the Baleste family, who later found another host family for my little sister. My mother joined the Resistance and suffered deeply during this period of her life. She repressed those memories and could never talk about them. According to my uncle, my Grandma Rivka was a wonderful woman: gentle, loving and ready to sacrifice herself for her loved ones. I am proud to be able to honor her in this book and to list her among the Resistance fighters. She is, in a way, my own Resistance fighter, nearest to my heart.

When war broke out, the Romanian Rivka Leiba lived on Rue des Panoyaux in the 20th arrondissement of Paris. Every day, she came to our apartment at 144 boulevard de Ménilmontant to take care of us, her two granddaughters, while our mother worked. My father was fighting in the French army. He died in the trenches in 1940, but my mother only learned of his death in 1942.

On September 24th, 1942, Romanian Jews were being rounded up throughout Paris. The French police came to the Rue des Panoyaux to arrest my grandmother and take her to Drancy. She was not home, but the concierge maliciously disclosed her whereabouts to the police, saying, "Rivka is at her daughter's house. You'll find her there." The horror of a collaborationist concierge who betrays you to the enemy!

Very soon, the doorbell rang at my mother's apartment. A loud knock and a booming voice resounded, "Police! Open up!"

Frightened, my grandmother immediately thought of her 19-year-old son, my uncle Daniel, who was with her. She bolted to push him into the farthest room, saying "Hide under the mattress!" My 2-year-old sister was eating in the kitchen, but the policeman ignored her. He ordered my grandmother to take a suitcase with some things, telling her she would be leaving for a few days. My grandmother had a sense of foreboding. She must, at all costs, avoid a search of the apartment, lest her young son be found. "Where I am going, I will need nothing," she retorted. Those were the last words my uncle heard his mother say. The policeman took Rivka to Drancy. Three days later, she arrived at the Bobigny train station and joined convoy 37 heading for Auschwitz. Two weeks later, she died in a gas chamber. Today, her name is among those of the deported at the Shoah Memorial.[102] She is immortal.

---

[102]*Memorial de la Shoah*, 17 rue Geoffroy Lasnier, 75004 Paris, France.

MEANS OF SURVIVAL

"Hold on until the end; never admit defeat. Even in death we shall be victorious. You shall walk, you shall work, you shall push human strength to its limits; beyond its limits. But preserve your dignity despite the blows, despite the waiting, despite the exhaustion."[103]

The heroism of these women is not an imitation of male heroism. It is their very own, female heroism. In our day and age, when the notion of gender equality has become part of the political discourse, it is important to honor that heroism by placing it in its unique historical context. These women had male role models, who inspired them to shape their own destiny as great French Resistance Fighters.

Far from being masculine, they were, quite simply, female paragons. They raised their femininity to its most exalted level. Their means of survival sprang from their inner strength as well as their physical energy and ingenuity. These women were united by their desire to preserve their human dignity and, at all costs, to do "something worthwhile," as one of them said, to defend France's honor and to defy the Occupation. They fashioned their own ethic.

Their mental and physical strength reached an all-time high, nurturing their perseverance and making it seem as if all of these women had the stamina for more than just fighting the enemy. Indeed, in addition to the battle against the occupying force, there raged within each of these women a battle against herself, against the fragility in which the society of men traditionally kept women locked. These Resistant Women's victory was thus a double one: military and psychological.

---

[103]Marie-Jo Chombart de Lauwe, *Toute une vie de résistance*, p. 62.

During one interrogation, Brigitte Friang hypnotized herself by staring at a clock on the wall so as not to react to the violent blows the guards inflicted upon her. Lucie Aubrac persevered for three months in order to obtain permission for her feigned marriage to the father of her unborn child. Despite the punishments she endured, Marie-Jo Chombart de Lauwe unrelentingly stood up to officers and prison guards. She continued to find new ways to communicate with the other women prisoners. In her book, she constantly emphasized the overarching need to fight. "We have fought for our just cause; we will fight to the end, and if we fall, it will be in combat, with dignity and pride."[104]

After her release from prison, Jacqueline Pardon was more determined than ever to pursue her activities. She left *Défense de la France* and became a secretary in a Maquis (guerilla movement). Marthe Cohn managed to join the French armed forces. When sent on a mission, she achieved the feat of joining the German army and gleaned valuable intelligence. Maïti Girtanner used the weapons of naïveté, audacity, tenacity and flattery to attain her goals.

These women feared nothing. They defied their adversaries in this complete internal, external, personal, patriotic and ideological combat, emerging even more impervious to pain and torture than men. When asked if she realized the gravity of her actions, Marie-Jo Chombart de Lauwe did not give in to her interrogators. She replied, "I am fully aware of it and I regret nothing"[105].

Their ingenious strategies for outwitting their captors revealed the astuteness of the feminine mind. Yvette Bernard Farnoux had

[104]*Ibid.* p. 58.
[105]*Ibid.* p. 49.

prisoners drink spoiled goat milk to make them sick and ensure their transfer to the hospital, from which it was easier to escape. Lucie Aubrac used the same stratagem, but with medicine, to get her husband out of prison. Marie-Jo Chombart de Lauwe and her mother sent each other messages written with lemon juice, which replaced invisible ink.

The women prisoners found various ways to communicate with those on the outside. They built their own tools to remove the nails sealing the windows of their cells. Marie-Jo Chombart de Lauwe and Noëlla Rouget communicated with their fellow prisoners by tapping messages on the wall and speaking through the pipes. To correspond with their families, they inserted messages into the hems of their clothing. Andrée Warlin wrote on a pink bra with thread of the same hue. In the babies' room at Ravensbrück, Marie-Jo and her companions used the fingers of rubber gloves as nipples for makeshift baby bottles.

At the Fresnes prison, Andrée Warlin wrapped her ring in brown wool and sewed it into the brim of her hat, which she sent to her sister. At Drancy, she hid weapons under the piano platform. When Marie-Jo Chombart de Lauwe was assigned the job of tuning radio switches for airplanes at the Ravensbrück Siemens factory, she and her companion worked as slowly as possible. "I spent hours doing my nails with a file and sandpaper."[106] In the Abteroda camp's rocket factory, Jacqueline Fleury mixed working and defective components. Brigitte Friang did the same in the Zwodau camp, while Henriette Kermann caused sawing machine breakdowns there by damaging the teeth of the saws.

---

[106]*Ibid.*, p. 73.

"Only solidarity allowed us to remain human when confronted with our executioners and their *schlague* beatings,"[107] wrote Raymonde Tillon. She and her companions did not hesitate to swap the Jewish star of the newly-deported for stolen red triangles marked with an F[108]. The women Resistance fighters rubbed each other's backs to keep warm during the long hours of roll call. They shared their meager bread rations with those who had been deprived of them as punishment. As a token of friendship, they made small gifts for each other out of leftover materials they found in the factories where they worked.

In transit, in the cattle wagons as well as in the camps, the youngest women helped the elderly and the sick. Those who could, tried to warn other women about raids that were in progress or planned. Jacqueline Pardon ran to the bookstore on the rue Bonaparte. Henriette Kermann and her group alerted the Jewish shop owners of Ménilmontant.

Brigitte Friang insisted on fraternity, which meant "firstly, facing death together."[109] She wondered, "Who will ever express the significance of fraternity in the camps, alongside the hate?"[110] The strong sense of community of these women Resistance fighters was born mainly of their maternal instinct.

Sometimes, a younger woman offered to replace an older, exhausted woman like Jacqueline Fleury's mother. Lou Peters came forward to receive a beating in Brigitte Friang's place, even though she barely knew her.

---

[107]*J'écris ton nom, Liberté*, p. 78.
[108]Letter designating one as French.
[109]She cites this phrase by Malraux in *Regarde-toi qui meurs*, p. 90.
[110]*Ibid.*, p. 198.

The prisoners exchanged advice on how best to bear the unbearable. Brigitte Friang and Marie-Jo Chombart de Lauwe declared that it was imperative to remain clean to keep one's dignity. Brigitte wrote, "A clean body is the symbol of refusing the slavery that they are trying to force upon us."[111] Bathing was, moreover, a source of great joy: "…washing in the small creek that winds through the vale. Despite the biting cold, what a delight to bare your skin and to clean it all over using gravel."[112] Marie-Jo emphasized the importance of hygiene even when one was dead tired. She recommended never treating oneself as a victim.

Both women made rules: "Never cry like an idiot. Never give up. Fight back."[113] "Never weaken despite the pain. Never become discouraged despite the agony."[114] They had indomitable strength of character. These women were guided by the light of their souls.

Brigitte and Marie-Jo were moved by nature's poetry, which gave them hope. During the "march of death," "we pass a lovely, clear forest of slender birches,"[115] wrote Brigitte. They were sensitive, vibrant. Their vitality was stronger than their hell.

In prison and in the camps, the Resistance fighters tried to find pleasant moments: the sight of a simple green plant outside, a ray of sunlight through the window, a conversation about meals they would relish, a song heard from a neighboring cell. Despite the war and its perversity, they preserved their natural love for life. Marie-Jo wrote, "Every day, I strive to find a pleasure, whether it

---

[111]*Ibid.*, p. 153.
[112]*Ibid.*, p. 198.
[113]*Regarde-toi qui meurs*, p. 96.
[114]*Ibid.*, p. 170.
[115]*Ibid.*, p. 176.

be a walk, a book, a good ration of bread, a broth that is not too transparent, or positive information. This almost always works. It is those things—usually so small—that we can seize in passing, that bring joy!"[116]

Daydreaming brought evasion. "Every morning, during roll call, we watch the sky to escape these horrors: I am the Big Dipper; it gallops with a sound of bells; my imagination takes me far, far away, towards the unreal."[117] Brigitte noticed "the stars [that] shimmer in a sky of ink,"[118] as she stood for three and a half hours in the freezing night.

On Sundays, the women met to sing or talk "about an issue, either in current events or philosophy, or something more general, such as responsibility or 'honor'."[119] At La Centrale, the main prison of Rennes, the women prisoners taught classes in subjects they knew. Henriette Kermann, who dropped out of school at a very young age, worked on her French.

Some of the women were actually able to laugh. Brigitte Friang pointed out its importance. She talked about fits of laughter as a way to release the pressure. "We burst out laughing. A loud, silly laughter, as overpowering as the fear we have felt."[120] Raymonde Tillon mentioned an episode that delighted her, when an officer fell out of his rocking chair during roll call: "Uncontrollable fits of laughter ran through our group despite the blows received from our jailers, infuriated by our audacity."[121] At

---

[116]*Toute une vie de résistance*, p. 41.

[117]*Ibid.* p. 82-3.

[118]*Ibid.* p. 178.

[119]*Regarde-toi qui meurs*, p. 105.

[120]*Regarde-toi qui meurs*, p. 39, as well as pp. 56, 57, 58, 73.

[121]*J'écris ton nom, Liberté*, p. 68.

the Santé prison, Marie-Jo exclaimed, "The French spirit always loves to laugh, even—and especially—here."[122]

When praised for their heroism, they downplay it: they consider what they did very natural and Lucie Aubrac even goes so far as to rectify the word: "it is not heroism; it is skill." Indeed, for all of these women, heroism is second nature. After all, it shares the traits of motherhood: sacrifice, generosity, endurance, patience. Does not the heroism of these great women patriots of the Resistance consist in giving life rather than giving up their own? All of these Resistance fighters had an ideal and, as they say, one cannot be a rebel without one.

Would I have had the courage, like Andrée Warlin, to admit to a group of strangers that I was Jewish? Could I have parted ways with my children in order to save them, as did my mother? Would I have been able to hide Jewish children, as did my Catholic host family?

The women that I interviewed are obviously not just women; they are exceptional women who were driven by uncommon circumstances to surpass their own limitations.

I often think of the grandness of these now venerable ladies I spoke with, of their humor, their boldness, their modesty, the valor of their past, which they see as something so "normal." On all fronts—as patriots, Resistance fighters, wives, mothers, sisters or friends, they carried the torch of hope. In the face of death, they vehemently affirmed their will to live. In the face of stupidity, their ingenuity surged. In the face of baseness, they rose to heroism.

---

[122]*Ibid.*, p. 36.

As a former hidden Jewish child, I would like to pass on this book in homage to new generations of women. Perhaps the actions of these remarkable foremothers will set an example for the younger generation. We must not be afraid to resist against the unacceptable. Over the course of these interviews, these heroines became, for me, a feminine incarnation of the Resistance. Listening to their memories makes us take pride in seeing the future of women through their eyes, and spurs us towards action. Under the spell of their inestimable achievements, we regain confidence in our capacity to resist against racism, anti-Semitism and attacks on freedom, and, above all, in our unique feminine ability to fight for the protection of those living around us.

ACKNOWLEDGMENTS

First and foremost, I would like to express my gratitude to the Resistance fighters who were kind enough to share their exemplary past with me: many thanks to Mrs. Aubrac, Mrs. Bohec, Mrs. Chombart de Lauwe, Mrs. Cohn, Mrs. Farnoux, Mrs. Fleury, Mrs. Friang, Mrs. Girtanner, Mrs. Kermann, Mrs. Klein-Leiber, Mrs. Pardon, Mrs. Prety, Mrs. Richet, Mrs. Rouget, Mrs. Tillon, Mrs. Viannay and Mrs. Warlin.

I want to thank my family, especially my grandmother, Rivka Leiba, and my sister Jacqueline Abrams.

A heartfelt thank you to Chantal Chawaf for her deep involvement in every stage of this project. She encouraged me and took painstaking care in editing my manuscript.

A big thank you also goes to Henri Weill.

Many thanks to Anna Krasnovsky-Quinard for her meticulous work and impeccable English translation from the original French.

Thank you to Pomona College for funding my trips to Paris and Melanie Sisneros for the formating of the text.

FRENCH HEROINES, 1940-1945

BIBLIOGRAPHY

Albrecht, Mireille. *Berty*. Paris: Robert Laffont, 1986.

Albrecht, Mireille. *Vivre au lieu d'exister*. Paris: éditions du Rocher, 2001.

Allison, Maggie. "From the Violence of War to the War against Intolerance: Representing the Resistant Woman, Lucie Aubrac.". *South Central Review* 19.4-20.1.

(Winter 2002- Spring 2003): 119-134.

Atack, Margaret. *Literature and the French Resistance*. Cultural politics and narrative forms, 1940-1950. Manchester and New York. Manchester University Press, 1989.

Aubrac, Lucie. *Ils Partiront dans l'ivresse*. Paris: Seuil, 1984.

Aubrac, Lucie. *Cette exigeante liberté: entretiens avec Corinne Bouchoux*, Paris: L'Archipel, 1997.

Baehrel, Sylvaine. *Alibi 1940-1944. Histoire d'un réseau de renseignement pendant la seconde guerre mondiale*. Paris: Jean-Michel Place, 2000.

Bédarida, Renée. *Les Armes de l'Esprit: Témoignage Chrétien, 1941-1944*, Paris: Les Editions Ouvrières, 1977.

Bertin, Celia. *Les femmes sous l'Occupation*. Paris: Stock, 1993.

Bertrand, Simone. *Mille visages, un seul combat: les femmes dans la résistance*. Paris: les Editeurs Français Réunis, 1965.

Block, Gay and Drucker, Malka. *Rescuers: of Moral Courage in the Holocaust*. Prologue by Cynthia Ozick. Afterword by Rabbi Harold M. Schulweis. New York. London. Holmes & Meier Publishers, Inc.

Bohec, Jeanne. *La Plastiqueuse à bicyclette*. Paris: éditions Du Félin, 1999.

Bood, Micheline. *Les Années Doubles: Journal d'une Lycéenne sous L'occupation*. Paris: Robert Laffont, 1974.

Boulineau, Annie et Chatel, Nicole. *Des Femmes dans la Résistance*. Paris: Julliard, 1972.

Bourdet, Claude. *L'aventure incertaine. De la Résistance à la restauration*. Paris: éditions du Félin, 1998.

Carré, Mathile-Lily. *J'ai été "La Chatte"*. Paris: éditions Morgan, 1959.

Chamming's, Marie. *J'ai choisi la tempête*. Paris: éditions France-Empire, 1965.

Cohn, Marthe and Holden, Wendy. *Behind Enemy Lines: the True Story of a French Jewish Spy in Nazi Germany*. New York: Harmony Books, 2002. Traductions: *Moi, Marthe juive et résistante derrière les lignes ennemies*. Paris: France-Loisirs 2004 et *Derrière les lignes ennemies: une espionne juive dans l'Allemagne nazie*. Traduction: Hélène Prouteau. Plon, 2004.

Coudert, Marie Louise. *Elles: la résistance*. Paris: Messidor, 1983.

De Lauwe, Chombard, Marie-Jo. *Toute une vie de Résistance*. Paris: éditions Graphein, 1998.

Delbo, Charlotte. *Le convoi de 14 janvier*. Paris: éditions de Minuit, 1965.

De l'Odéon, Monique. *Une jeune femme condamnée à mort*. Paris: Tallandier, 2002.

Delpla, François. *Aubrac: les faits et la calomnie*. Paris: Le Temps des Cerises, 1997.

Diamant, David. *La Résistance Juive entre gloire et tragédie*. Paris: L'Harmattan, 1993.

Fabius, Odette. *Un lever de soleil sur le Mecklembourg*. Paris: Albin Michel, 1986.

Femmes dans la guerre. collectif. Paris: éditions du Félin, 2004.

Fourcade, Maric-Madeleine. *L'arche de Noé*. Paris: Plon, 1989.
Francos, Ania. *Il était des femmes dans la résistance*. Paris: Stock, 1978.

Friang, Brigitte. *Regarde-toi qui meurs*. Paris: éditions du Félin, 1997.

Gilzmer Mechtild, Levisse-Touzé Christine, Martens, Stefan. *Les femmes dans la Résistance en France.* Paris: Tallandier, 2003.

Girtaner, Maïti. *Résistance et pardon.* Paris: Vie Chrétienne, 2003.

Gold, Mary Jane. *Marseille Année 40.* Paris: Phébus, 2001.

Granet, Marie. *Défense de la France. Histoire d'un Mouvement de Résistance* (1940-1944). Paris: Presses Universitaires de France, 1960.

Granet, Marie. *Les femmes dans la résistance: 20 ans en 1940.* Paris: France Empire, 1996.

Grynberg, Annne. *Les Camps de la honte.* Paris: La Découverte, 1991.

Guidez, Guylaine. *Femmes dans la guerre 1939-45.* Paris: Perrin, 1989.

Jeannin-Garreau, Eliane. *Ombre parmi les ombres: Chronique d'une Résistante 1941-1945.* Issy-les-Moulineaux: éditions Muller, 1991.

Kaspi, André, Kriegel, Annie et Wieviorka, Annette (dir.). *Les Juifs de France dans la seconde guerre mondiale.* Paris: Cerf, 1992.

Kedward, Roderick and Austin, Roger (dir). *Vichy France and the Résistance. Culture and Ideology.* London & Sydney. Croom Helm, 1985.

Kermann, Henriette. *La Résistance que j'ai faite, la déportation que j'ai vécue*. Paris: FNDIRP, 1991.

Knibiehler, Yvonne. *Nous les Assistantes Sociales*. Paris: éditions Aubier Montaigne, 1980.

Kriegel, Annie. *Ce que j'ai cru comprendre*. Paris: Robert Laffont, 1991.

Langlois, Caroline et Reynaud, Michel. *Elles et Eux dans la résistance*. Paris: Tiresias, 2003.

Laska, Vera. *Women in the Resistance and in the Holocaust: the voices of Eyewitnesses*. Wesport. Conn: Greenwood Press, 1983.

Latour, Anny. *La Résistance juive en France*. Paris: Stock, 1970. Lazare, Lucien. *La Résistance juive en France*. Paris: Stock, 1987.

Le Tac, Yvonne. *Une Femme dans le siècle*. Paris: éditions Tiresias, 2000.

Le Trividic, Dominique Martin. *Une héroïne de la Résistance*. Les Sables-d'Olonne. Ed. Le Cercle d'Or, 1979. Rennes: éditions Ouest-France,2002.

Malraux, André. *Antimémoires. "Le miroir des Limbes I"*. Paris: Gallimard, 1972.

Martin-Chauffier, Simone. *A bientôt quand même*. Paris: Calmann-Lévy, 1976.

Monestier, Marianne. *Elles étaient cent et mille*. Paris: Fayard, 1972.

Montagnard, Julie et Picar, Michel. *Danielle Mitterand: Portrait*. Paris: éditions Ramsay, 1982.

Moreau, Emilienne. *La Guerre Buissonnière*. Paris: Solar Editeur, 1970.

Moskovitz, Sarah. *Love Despite Hate: Child Survivors of the Holocaust and their Adult Lives*. New York: Schocken Books, 1983.

Noguères, Henri. *La vie quotidienne des Résistants de l'armistice à la Libération*. Paris: Hachette, 1984.

Ousoulias-Romagon. *J'étais agent de liaison des F.T.P.T*. Paris: éditions Messidor, 1988.

Perrot, Michelle. *Les Femmes ou les silence de l'Histoire*. Paris: Flammarion, 1998.

Poznanski, Renée. *Les Juifs en France pendant la Seconde Guerre mondiale*. Paris: Hachette, 1997.

Riffaud, Madeleine. *On l'appelait Rainer*. Paris: Julliard, 1994.

Robert, Jeanne et Michèle. *Le Réseau Victoire dans le Gers*. Paris: Alam Sutton, 2003.

Rotman, Michèle. *Carnets de mémoires. Enfances cachées 1939-1945*. Paris: Ramsay, 2005.

Terrenoire, Elisabeth. *Les femmes dans la Résistance: Combattantes sans uniformes*. Paris: Bloud & Gay, 1946.

Tillon, Raymonde. *J'écris ton nom, Liberté*. Paris: éditions du Félin, 2002.

Une femme résistante. Dir. Jean Michel Barjol. Images Marguerite Gonon, 1991.

Union des Femmes Françaises. *Les Femmes dans la Résistance (Colloque)*. Paris: éditions du Rocher, 1977.

Viannay, Philippe. *Du bon usage de la France*. Paris: éditions Ramsay,1988.

Warlin, Andrée. *L'impossible oubli*. Paris: La pensée universelle, 1980.

Weitz, Margaret. *Sisters in the Resistance: How Women Fought to Free France*. New York: John Wiley & Sons, Inc. 1995.

Zeitoun, Sabine. *Ces enfants qu'il fallait sauver*. Paris: Albin Michel, 1989.

French Heroines, 1940-1945